Memories
from a
Life
Well Lived

BY HERMAN SILVERMAN

Ben Silver

*To Eli – a good friend and
great Doctor*

ISBN-10: 1500287490 (paperback)
ISBN 13: 9781500287498

Library of Congress Control Number: 2014911490
CreateSpace Independent Publishing Platform
North Charleston, South Carolina

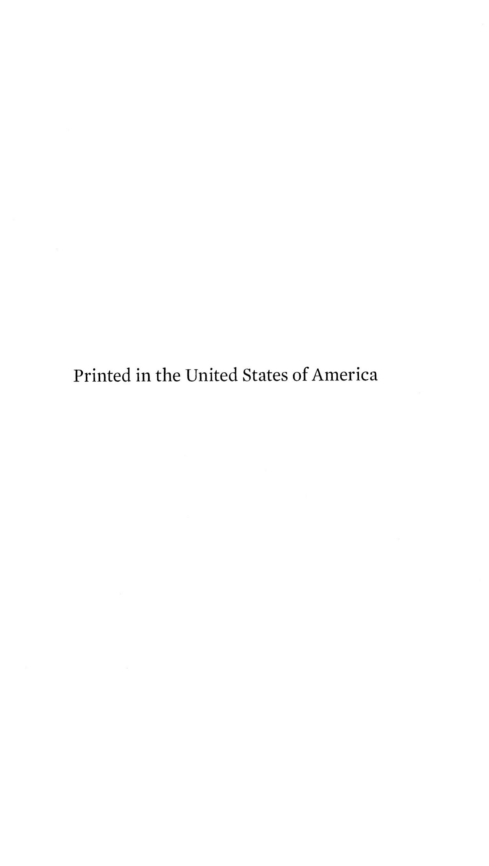

This book is dedicated to
my family
and in loving memory of
my wife Ann
and my brothers, Sidney and Ira.

Also by Herman Silverman
Michener and Me
Mergentwerker
(illustrated by Roy McKie)

Acknowledgments

To my wife Liz Serkin: my heartfelt appreciation for all you did in helping me write a memoir that reflects who I am, what I have learned, and what matters most to me.

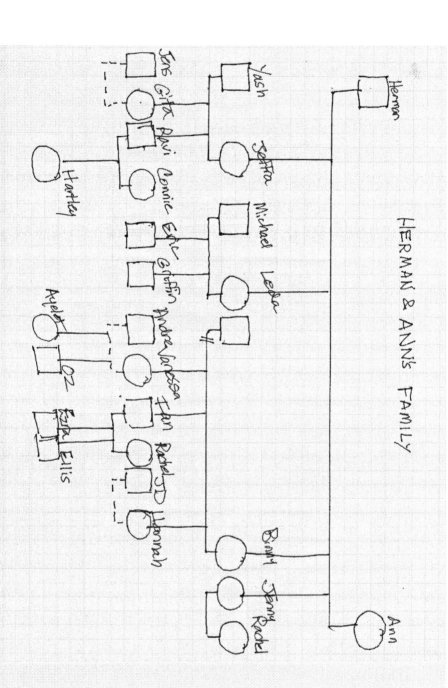

HERMAN & ANN'S FAMILY

Memories from a Life Well Lived

CONTENTS

CHAPTER 1

My First Miracle

It is the first of the three miracles that I am alive.

What I am about to tell you was how my mother told me it was; I cannot verify it.

It wasn't supposed to happen quite the way it did. On January 4, 1920, a cold, snowy day in Camden, an industrial city across the Delaware River from Philadelphia, I'm trying hard to be born. My mother, Elizabeth, sometimes called Liz, is struggling, my father is pacing the hallway, and the midwife is worried.

The midwife directs my father to get us to the hospital. Fast. He learns there are no ambulances available, because all of them are already out on emergency calls due to the snow and ice. My father is frantic. He calls the police, who venture out in a paddy wagon to pick up a doctor at the hospital and then drive to our house to pick up my mother, the midwife, and "me." The paddy wagon, designed to transport prisoners, has long benches in the back. My mother lies down on one of these long seats.

We don't make it to the hospital in time. The doctor and the midwife deliver me en route in the paddy wagon. Later, the doctor tells my parents that there was a good chance that I wouldn't have survived my birth. The delivery was complicated, and having to deliver me in a speeding paddy wagon, bouncing and shaking along rutted streets through a snowstorm, made it even more difficult.

I think my being born this way is one of the reasons I'm always in a hurry.

Today Camden, New Jersey, is one of the poorest and most dangerous cities in the United States. But Camden does have bragging rights: it was the where Walt Whitman died, where the Campbell Soup Company was established, and where I, Herman Silverman, was born.

CHAPTER 2

My Parents and Their Families

My mother, Elizabeth Bendesky, came from Kiev. Her house in the *shtetl* had a dirt floor; in the winter the farm animals lived in the house to keep the family from freezing. If you've seen *Fiddler on the Roof,* you have an idea of what it was like.

The family was fleeing the Cossacks, soldiers of the czar, who would threaten the Jews, extort money from them, and worse. My mother was lucky because her brother Abe Ben had immigrated to America and sent her money to follow him here. It was a long, difficult journey. She crossed Europe to a port where she caught a ship. She traveled under horrible conditions in steerage, and the crossing lasted ten days.

She ended up in Camden, New Jersey, where she met my father. Family tradition has her as a very attractive young woman, always concerned about her appearance, a stylish dresser. She had little education, but her mind was lively, and she was interested in everything around her. She was fluent in four languages: her native Russian, Yiddish, English, and a combination of those three, used when she was excited or angry.

From what I heard growing up, my mother was a person who knew how to get along in the world. After our father died, she successfully raised the three of us, all of us turning out pretty good. One thing she would say to us that I never forgot, warning us to stay out of trouble, speaking in her fourth language, was "A *shonda* for the neighbors," meaning that we must never do anything that could make her feel ashamed. We followed that rule pretty carefully, and I think it had a positive impact on how we turned out as adults.

My mother's brother Abe, the one who brought her over, a rough kind of guy, was a master carpenter who became a subcontractor to some developers in Northeast Philadelphia. He smoked a lot and always smelled of cigarettes. His moustache was yellow from the tobacco. Abe never smiled, but I remember him as being very nice to us. He owned one of the few Chevrolets around, a 1929 or 1930 four-door sedan. He would take us for rides in the country. Later, he would help us move from Pottstown to Philadelphia, helping us out financially until we were settled.

Abe's wife was very different from Abe. She seemed bitter, an impression I had even as a kid. According to my mother, Abe's wife resented his kindness and generosity toward us, afraid he would give us more money than she thought necessary. Their daughters, my cousins—Minnie, Ethel, and Ruth—were more like their father. They helped us any way they could and always made us feel welcome.

One thing Uncle Abe did for us that I will never forget was his building us a hot dog stand. It was during the Depression, our father had died, and we needed to supplement the money we were getting from Mother's Assistance and various charities. The stand was four feet wide and eight feet long, with a couple of panels in the front that opened up. My mother sold hot dogs, sodas, candy, and snacks to the men who worked on Uncle Abe's construction sites. He also set me up with a wagon loaded with the same foodstuffs. And I would walk through the housing developments, peddling my wares—"Hear ye! Hear ye! Sodas! Candy! Hot dogs!" I would do this every day when I wasn't in school, while my mother and brother Sid took care of the stand.

My father, Samuel Silverman, was two years older than my mother and twenty when they got married. I know very little about him or his family. He died when I was nine years old in a flu epidemic. I know he came from a small town in Lithuania, crossed the Atlantic, and ended up in Camden. He was a paperhanger. I don't have many memories of him, but I think he must have been a nice guy and a good businessman. He was able to buy a Ford Model T truck, hire a helper, and provide a good living for the family. There's a picture of him in a Russian costume and in a band, where he is holding a mandolin.

My father was forty-three when he died. He'd been admitted to Pottstown Hospital with pneumonia. Back then, when a patient ran a high fever, it was called "the crisis," and the only treatment was to wrap cold, wet sheets around him or her. If the fever didn't drop, the patient died.

My mother was with my father at the hospital. My brothers and I waited at home. When we hadn't heard from her for five hours, my brother Sid, the oldest brother at age twelve, called the hospital and asked the operator about Sam Silverman.

"Sam Silverman?" she responded. "He died an hour ago."

Had he lived, I probably would have become a paperhanger, because in those days boys almost always took up their father's profession, first as a helper, then as a partner, and eventually as owner of the business.

Uncle Bill, my father's brother, gave us a little money at our father's funeral and three years later invited my brother Sid and me to spend the summer with him and his wife, Aunt Dora, in Bayshore, Long Island, about forty miles from New York City. They had no children and were glad to have us. Bill owned a stationery store, where he sold cigarettes, cigars, newspapers, magazines, and fancy writing paper. He also took bets on the horse races, a lucrative side business, because, as the local bookie, he took a cut of every bet.

Uncle Bill and Aunt Dora lived in an apartment above the store. Every morning Bill would go to the barber for a shave, costing twenty-five cents. Then he would open the store, where Sid and I would work in the mornings and then go to the beach for the afternoons. Customers would call the store to place their bets or come in to buy boxes of expensive cigars or cigarettes at twenty-five cents for two packs. The business thrived.

My father and Bill had another sibling, Bessie, who was about ten years younger than Bill. During the Depression, with jobs as hard to find as husbands, Bill gave Bessie's husband a job in his store.

Bessie was at least forty when she married. I never liked her husband Harry, an unpleasant fellow who always had a cigar in his mouth. I thought he was a no-good bum. He and Bessie moved into an apartment across the street, and he worked for Bill for about a year, getting to know the business and the customers.

Then overnight, without saying anything to Bill, he opened a store right across the street. He assumed the customers he'd met while working for Bill would follow him, but not one of Bill's customers left him, and after a year or so, the no-good bum had to close his shop. Aunt Dora and Uncle Bill were deeply hurt and never talked about Bessie's husband again.

Later, after Aunt Dora died, Uncle Bill sold the store for a nice profit and opened another one in nearby Huntington

Station, where Sid and I would visit him and his second wife.

Bill had a way of making his customers like him. They called him by his first name, and he always acted toward them as though they were friends, as I believe he actually considered them to be. I learned a lot from watching him interact with customers. I give him credit for the relationships I later developed with people who bought my swimming pools, relationships that lasted long after I was no longer in that business.

CHAPTER 3

....

Sid and Izzy

I had two brothers: Sid was three years older than I, and Ira, whom we called Izzy, was six years younger than I. Sid, born on Christmas Day 1917 in Philadelphia, was always a good friend to Izzy and me.

When we moved back to Philadelphia after our father died, Sid took the corner of Thirty-Third Street and York Avenue to sell the *Bulletin* and the evening edition of the *Inquirer*. He and I would wait at the corner around five o'clock every afternoon until a truck would come by and the driver would throw bundles of papers to us. I don't know how Sid got that corner—a good spot for selling papers, because it was at a traffic light.

Whenever a car stopped for the light, Sidney would run to the driver's window and hand him a paper. Meanwhile, I would take about twenty papers, carrying them in a bag with a strap over my shoulder, and walk down the street, shouting, "Extra, extra. Read all about it," just like in the movies. The customer would give us three cents; we would get seven-eighths of a cent for every paper we sold. Both Sid and I gave all our earnings to our mother.

Sid later added to the family income by playing his saxophone. As a student at Central High, he joined the music class and took up the saxophone, learning to play well enough to form a band with five of his classmates and playing at weddings and other events.

When Sid graduated from Central, there was no possibility of going to college. He took a job at Lit Brothers, a department store in Philadelphia, making enough money that I didn't have to take a job myself when I had the opportunity to go to Farm School after my own graduation from Central.

Sid fell in love with Ruth. They married before he was drafted. After his discharge from the army, Ruth's father gave him a job in a liquor store he owned in New Jersey. Sid wasn't happy in that job and went on to sell special light bulbs, becoming the number-one salesman for the company and eventually buying it and building up the business into a successful electrical supply company.

Sid and Ruth had two sons, Stanley and Stewart, both of whom graduated from Drexel University and became successful in their own right.

On retirement Ruth and Sid bought a beautiful house on the Jersey Shore and sold their house in Philadelphia. The night after the closing on their Philadelphia house, when they were spending the night in a hotel before planning to move into their new home the next day, Ruth found her husband on the bathroom floor, dead of a stroke. It was a terrible loss to all of us.

I don't have many memories of Izzy while we were growing up. I didn't spend much time with him, being six years older.

Being Jewish, we didn't celebrate Christmas, but of course we knew all about Santa Claus. One Christmas Eve, when Izzy was about three, I got hold of a bag of candy canes. After he went to sleep, I laid the candy canes on the windowsill next to his bed. In the morning when he woke up, I told him Santa had left them for him. It was a joy to see how happy and excited he was.

Izzy was smart and a good student. He went to Central High, as Sid and I had done. After Izzy graduated, our mother married a nice fellow and moved to Queens. My wife Ann and I asked Izzy to live with us. Izzy had dreams of becoming a doctor, but we had no money for medical school tuition. He found out about scholarships available to poor students to attend the Philadelphia College of Optometry, and so Izzy became an optometrist.

(Thirty years later, Izzy became the chairman of the college's board of directors and was a major contributor.)

I rented an office for him in Doylestown and outfitted it with everything he would need to set up his practice. In those days there were only one other optometrist and three dentists in town. He was building his clientele when it became clear he would be drafted into the Korean War. Our good friend Dr. Cooperman, one of the three dentists in Doylestown, helped Izzy get assigned to the army medical corps.

Izzy was stationed at a military base about fifty miles from Tokyo. One day he followed an American girl when she got off a bus; that was how Izzy met Mattiemae. They married, and I convinced him to forget about being an optometrist and to go into the pool business with me. We became partners, and he was very important to the success of Sylvan Pools.

Izzy and Mattiemae lived in a beautiful stone farmhouse only a mile or so from Ann and me. They came to family events, such as birthdays and weddings, and stayed with our daughters when Ann and I would travel to Europe without them, but mostly we socialized with different sets of friends.

Izzy and I met every week to discuss the Sylvan Pools business over lunch at Conti's, the family's favorite restaurant. Our partnership worked, as I was mostly responsible for the financial part and he for the part that required people skills. Everyone loved Izzy.

When Izzy retired, Souderton Bank asked him to sit on the board of a large company that built and ran high-end retirement developments. He found out after joining the board that the company's finances weren't in order. He came up with a plan to turn the company around and was appointed board president.

One day in a board meeting, he complained of a terrible headache and dropped his head on the table. He was rushed by ambulance to the Doylestown hospital, where

Mattiemae, Ann, and I, hoping for a miracle, kept vigil while Ira was in intensive care. Two days later Izzy was gone, dead of a stroke.

Izzy had arranged for his body to be cremated. Mattiemae kept his ashes in a shoe box until she, Ann, and I scattered them around their farm.

I still tear up when I think about him. I think about him every day. I miss him terribly.

Izzy's death was unexpected and left me wondering why. We all know that strokes are hereditary. Both our mother and Sid had died of strokes. And now there was Izzy, who'd lived a clean, healthy life and never smoked, never drank alcohol, walked every day the miles around Lake Galena, was a practicing Quaker, and had wonderful relationships with many people. And here I am, the only survivor of my original family, about to celebrate my ninety-fifth birthday, still alive and healthy.

I sometimes wonder also about how my brothers and I grew up to be the men we became. In part, I think it was because the three of us took care of each other. I also give credit to our mother, a Jewish immigrant who never fully assimilated, keeping semikosher, speaking Yiddish in the home, and always cooking a big chicken dinner on Fridays. She had very little influence on our lives beyond our home, however.

CHAPTER 4

....

Bris

Being born a male child to Jewish parents, of course, I had a *bris*. Had I been born today, I probably would have been circumcised in a hospital, with a surgeon performing the operation, but in 1920 Jewish baby boys had a ritual circumcision in the parents' home, with a specialist, called a mohel, performing the surgery.

Here is how I assume my bris proceeded. I think my parents chose a mohel of good reputation, most likely paying a premium price to employ a mohel known for inflicting a minimum of pain on the baby. Family and friends would have been invited to the house—men in the living room with me, my father and the mohel and the women in the dining room, drinking tea and eating cake and gossiping.

My father would have carried me into the living room on a pillow and laid me on a table covered with a special cloth. The men would have gathered around. The mohel would have said a prayer: "Blessed is the one who has arrived." The mohel probably gave me sugar water or wine to quiet me down and then carefully cut off my foreskin. The guests would then have drunk a congratulatory toast to my father: mazel tov! More blessings, more wine, and I was given my Hebrew name, Haim.

I'm happy that my parents picked a good mohel. Accuracy is important. One wrong cut, and I could have grown up peeing sideways.

CHAPTER 5

Pottstown Years

We moved to Pottstown, because I burned down my father's store and our apartment above the shop. They said I started the fire, but how can I be sure? I was only five years old.

My father, mother, Sid, and I had moved from Camden to Philadelphia, where my father had opened a paperhanging store. He worked day and night, and built a successful business. In those days people didn't paint the rooms in their houses; they papered them. Customers would come into the shop to choose their paper, and my father would prepare their purchases and then hang the paper for them.

Preparing the paper involved putting the rolls through a trimming machine, which cut off the protective edges. These endpieces would wind up in a large box. For some reason my parents said it was because I was playing with matches. The paper caught fire, and soon the whole shop and house were burning.

We lived next door to a firehouse. My father ran, hollering, into the street, and the firemen responded right away. They didn't even take the truck out, as we were right next door; they just unrolled the hoses off the truck and put out the fire. But there was too much damage, and we had to move.

Fortunately, we had family in Pottstown. Uncle Gussman was my mother's cousin, not really our uncle, but he helped us move and settle in. I remember him as a good guy. He would have been about fifty then. He owned a men's store and also a prospering real estate business. He suggested my father go back into the paperhanging business, renting an empty store on the main business street.

Above the store was an apartment with two bedrooms, one for my parents and one for Sid and me—and within the year also for Izzy—plus a bathroom. Downstairs behind the shop was a large kitchen, where we spent much of our time. I don't remember a living room.

Our Uncle Gussman would sometimes take me with him when he would go out, collecting rent from the tenants in the farmhouses he owned. I became aware that money transactions can mean more than a transfer of money, as I saw his tenants give him eggs or butter along with the rent. Everyone loved Uncle Gussman.

Pottstown was a small manufacturing town. The main street was about four blocks long. There were no parks or playgrounds, and mostly we played in the alley behind the shop, a large driveway where trucks made their deliveries.

Next door to us was a store that sold floor coverings; five children lived above the store and played in our alley with us.

We also played on the wall around the Hill School, a school for rich kids, whom I knew we'd never meet. The wall started at three feet and wound up at least ten feet high. Of course we could have gotten hurt or killed, but it was lots of fun to walk along the wall.

One of the boys, a teenager, fascinated me. We called him "Peggy" because he had a wooden leg. It was awesome to watch him play basketball with the other boys in our neighborhood.

Another kid I knew was the son of a junk dealer. His father would go around town with a horse and wagon, picking up whatever junk he could find: old wheels, pieces of metal, cans, an old boiler. The junkyard was close to town. The Jewish townspeople ostracized the family, because being in the junk business was considered inappropriate and improper for a Jewish man.

The irony is that the son who was my age, a classmate in Hebrew school when we were very young, became one of the most successful junk dealers in the country. You can see some of his big machines on the way to the Philadelphia airport, machines that lift automobiles, put them on a belt, and then chop them into little pieces.

One incident I remember from our Pottstown years was when a man opened up his coat in front of us and exposed himself. We all screamed and hollered. The police eventually came and took the poor guy away.

Near the alley behind our house was a small shed where a man rolled cigars. He also played the drum and gave lessons. My father thought I should learn to play the drum, and this man taught me, first with two sticks and later on a snare drum.

My father was a musician. People tell me he was a very good violin player, and he was proficient in several other instruments. I have seen a photograph of him, dressed in a Cossack uniform, sitting on the floor in front of a band that played guitars and mandolins.

Pottstown had a close-knit Jewish community, with a very nice synagogue right on the main street. I have memories of going to the synagogue for high holidays, and I did go to Hebrew school there, because it was expected, but I never did get into observing Jewish rituals and practices.

Izzy was born in Pottstown. My father died in Pottstown. After he died, everything changed. In my memory it was then that I realized I was on my own, which is strange because even as a young child before my father died, I had felt I was on my own. With my father working so hard, he had little time for me, and my mother was preoccupied with her traditional roles in caring for us and the home.

But that also was when we three brothers realized we had each other, and we did have relatives who tried to help, as they had when my father set up his business. My father's brother came to the funeral. I do remember him giving some money to my mother. I don't remember anything about the funeral, and I have no memory of going to the cemetery. It's all a blur. I don't even know whether or where my father was buried.

I have mostly happy memories of Pottstown, of the kids I played with in the alleys, of the Fourth of July parade, of our life there. It was good until my father died.

That is when everything changed. We were virtually penniless. I'm quite sure my father hadn't taken out a life insurance policy. But we had cousins and other relatives in Philadelphia offering to help. A cousin, Morris Swersky and his family, allowed us to live in their home until my mother could get set up for us to have our own place. That is how we left Pottstown and moved to Philadelphia.

CHAPTER 6

Bar Mitzvah

My brother Sid had his bar mitzvah when he was thirteen. He'd spent months studying with a rabbi and a Hebrew teacher, preparing for the event. Sid sat on the bima, was led to the table holding the Torah, read from the Torah as required, made a ten-minute speech, in which he spoke of the verses he had read, and thanked our mother.

My mother didn't have money for a party. After the service one Saturday morning, she invited the people there to come to a small room in the basement of the synagogue, where she served sponge cake, seltzer, and some whiskey. It was a simple event.

When it was my turn at thirteen, I flatly refused to have a bar mitzvah. I was in a rebellious stage and wanted nothing to do with religion. No way was I going to spend months studying with a rabbi, nor would I get up in front of a large crowd on a Saturday morning and go through the whole rigmarole of becoming a man. I'd endured a few years of Hebrew school in Pottstown, and that was enough.

But Sid, my mother, and some relatives put so much pressure on me that we finally reached a compromise. The family reminded me that unless you are bar mitzvahed you cannot be recognized as a Jew. I hadn't given any thought to whether I even wanted to be recognized as a Jew, but of course I knew that I was one, so I agreed to have a bar mitzvah, but I held out for my terms.

Forget the religious preparation and forget the idea of a large audience. And there would absolutely be no party afterward. I agreed to make it official on a Wednesday morning at 10:00 a.m. when there would be the required minion of ten Jewish men. Sid brought me to the synagogue. I read a few lines from the Torah and was pronounced a Jewish man.

No party meant no gifts. Six years later, it was my younger brother Izzy's turn. My mother, who was very smart, figured out how she could raise money through Izzy's bar mitzvah. She approached a low-cost Jewish restaurant in the neighborhood and arranged a post-bar mitzvah banquet, for which she would pay about five or maybe ten dollars a person. She invited all the relatives and friends she could think of, knowing they would each bring at least fifty dollars, some even one hundred dollars. During lunch, as Izzy walked around the restaurant, people stuffed money into his pockets. My mother cleared a couple of thousand dollars.

CHAPTER 7

Living in Philadelphia

We came to Philadelphia, penniless. My mother's nephew, a successful banana merchant named Morris Swersky, took us into his beautiful home. His four daughters doubled up to give us two bedrooms. The family took care of us, the poor immigrant relatives from Pottstown, Morris's widowed aunt and her three children. We knew we were a burden on the Swersky family, and after three or four months we moved into a tiny house nearby. Soon afterward we rented the third floor in a house in the Strawberry Mansion section of Philadelphia.

It was 1929, the heart of the Depression. It actually helped to be a family without a husband and father. As fatherless children, we were considered orphans. Our family was eligible for Mother's Assistance and other benefits. The government gave us eight dollars a month to pay our rent, and Jewish Charities provided medical care and a wonderful social worker, Mrs. Krause, who helped our mother with any crisis that came up.

We were able to make ends meet, with Sid and me selling papers, and our mother selling coal door-to-door. People would take pity on the poor widow and order two or three sacks. Our mother would call the orders into the coal company. The coal company would deliver the coal in big canvas bags, each holding about fifty pounds. Two big, strong men would empty the bags for each customer through a basement window into a coal bin. As soon as the coal had been delivered, our mother would collect the money owed and take it to the coal company owners. She was paid fifteen cents a bag, maybe twenty-five, making four or five dollars on a good day. This was actually quite good at a time when most people, lucky enough to work, were making forty-eight cents an hour.

We also were very lucky to get first-rate medical care. Jewish Charities assigned an excellent gynecologist to take care of our mother and a fine family doctor to take care of my brothers and me. We boys would have appointments with him in his elegant Center City offices, but he also made house calls. I remember one time when I had a fever and our mother called him at eight o'clock at night.

The doctor lived way out on the Main Line, and it must have been inconvenient to make a late-night house call, but there he was, elegantly dressed. I stared at his monogrammed silver cuff links and decided that I would make enough money to afford elegant clothes.

And someday I would have an apartment on Rittenhouse Square like the one our social worker, a wealthy woman, lived in. This woman befriended my mother in ways social workers no longer do. She gave my mother her husband's old suits, which my mother could cut down for us, and we even had lunch with her in her apartment.

I developed a personal frame of reference for what it would be like to live the life of a wealthy man. This frame of reference went beyond the Rittenhouse Square and Main Line lifestyles to include philanthropy and service to others. I elaborated on my fantasy by reading the society column of the *Philadelphia Bulletin*. It was also at that time that I became even more aware that I was on my own, that if I was going to be successful, I would have to do it myself.

Meanwhile, life in Strawberry Mansion was great. Nobody had any money, but we had good times. There was almost every kind of business in the neighborhood, in an area only about ten blocks long and five blocks wide. I remember two bakeries, a butter-and-egg store, a hardware store, a shop that sold women's brassieres, and a shoe store. It was like a small town.

In the summer we would go to the end of Thirty-Third Street, the main street, to an establishment called Cherry's and order "glaciers," the scrapings off a block of ice placed in a paper cone and doused with all kinds of syrup. I find that snow cones today don't taste as good as these glaciers.

Most probably because of the emphasis on education and hard work, many of us who grew up in Strawberry Mansion went on to college and to successful careers in politics, medicine, the law, and academia.

The neighborhood was next to Fairmount Park, where there was a pavilion for concerts on summer Sundays, well-maintained tennis courts, and a free swimming pool.

The pool wasn't large enough for everyone who wanted to swim on hot summer days, so the pool directors scheduled hourly sessions, with boys and girls swimming either in the morning or in the afternoon. The pool could accommodate about fifty kids at a time. We would wait our turn in a large anteroom with rows of benches lining the walls.

In theory we were allowed only one hour a day in the pool. The staff kept track of who'd had their turn by checking our bathing suits to see whether they were wet or dry. None of us owned a second bathing suit, so to get a second swim in the pool, we would have to dry out our suits. We did this by laying our wet suits flat in the street and counting on passing cars to run over them and squeeze out the water. Then we would lay them in the sun on the pavement. Sometimes this would work, and we could get back in the pool.

There was a second pool in the park about five miles from where we lived, a large one with a high dive and a slide. It cost ten cents for a whole day. You could take a park trolley for a nickel, but we mostly walked to save the five cents.

For twenty cents for the day, we could rent a canoe or rowboat to take on the Schuykill River, which ran along the park. In winter we had great sledding. And it was in

Fairmount Park, when I was in my teens, that I made out for hours with a girl named Patty.

Let me tell you about our home. We had three bedrooms on the top floor and shared a bathroom on the second floor with the owners of the house, our landlords and their two lovely daughters, who lived below us. What I remember best is how I liked the way these young women smelled and how I felt when one of them would let me brush up against her when we passed in the narrow stairs.

In bad weather the young women would string lines in the bathroom to hang their underwear to dry. My appreciation for beautiful women's lingerie had its beginnings in that bathroom, and it was during this time, when I was in my very early teens, that I discovered how much I liked the feelings I got when sniffing the underwear, touching the girls on the stairs, and spying on the daughter who would entertain her boyfriend behind the house.

I often think about how much of my life had its beginnings in Philadelphia. On weekends I would go with two or three friends to the Philadelphia Museum of Art and the Rodin Museum. My love of art grew out of the experiences of looking at beautiful paintings at the museum and at the incredible sculpture at the Rodin. We also would cross the street to the Academy of Natural Sciences, where the exhibits fascinated us.

I enjoyed school, although I don't remember much before I graduated from eighth grade. Most of my classmates were going to Gratz High School, and I assumed I would go there as well, looking forward to being with my friends. But my school counselor said, "Herman, you are going to Central High." I argued with her, but of course I ended up at Central, where my brother Sidney was a senior. It was the best thing that could have happened to me, because I got the most excellent education that I could have gotten anywhere.

Central High was the kind of school where one spent an entire semester studying *Hamlet*. We studied physics, drafting, languages, math, history, literature, and more. It was here, especially in my Shakespeare classes, that I discovered a love of learning and developed a curiosity that all my life has led me to learn as much as I can in many, many areas. I didn't go to college—it never occurred to me that I probably could have won scholarships and continued my education in college, although almost all classmates did go to college and became professionals.

Those Philadelphia years were also when I learned at a young age to become an entrepreneur. Selling newspapers; my first jobs; certain opportunities to make money; the support of my brother Sid; the examples of Uncle Abe, Uncle Bill, Morris Swersky, and others; and some very good luck resulted in my later considerable successes as an entrepreneur.

CHAPTER 8

My Second Miracle

We were living on Page Street in the Strawberry Mansion neighborhood in Philadelphia in our third-floor apartment. I was eleven, and Izzy was five. We were playing tag, chasing each other around the four rooms of our apartment. I was eating a peach while running. Not a good idea.

My mother noticed I was choking and turning blue. She rushed to the window and started screaming for help. Lucky for me, our milkman was right there at the curb with his horse and wagon. He ran up the three flights of stairs, where I was turning darker blue every moment. He threw me over his shoulder and hurried down the stairs to carry me to the doctor's office on the corner of the block. My belly was bouncing against his shoulder as he raced down the stairs. I vividly remember the peach pit flying out of my throat and calling to my mother, "I'm all right, Mom."

In those days, since we didn't yet have refrigeration—only iceboxes—milk would be delivered to our door each morning. We would leave the empty bottles outside the door every night, with a note indicating any changes in our milk order or additions, such as cream or chocolate milk.

The milkman just happened to be collecting from his customers in front of our house that day. He could have been anywhere on our street or on another street. That he was on hand to save my life at that exact moment was my second miracle.

I'm sure my mother thanked him. I don't remember whether I did.

But fast-forward!

Over the years I often thought about the milkman and wished I could find out where he was so that I could thank him appropriately. One day, decades after the fact, a pamphlet came across my desk featuring my old neighborhood, Strawberry Mansion, and there it was, a full-page picture of the milkman with his horse and wagon, listing his name in the caption. Harry Himmel himself! I set about to find out whether he had any children or grandchildren I could contact.

My secretary, Barbara, found ten Himmels in the Philadelphia phone book. I wrote to all of them, asking whether they had a father or grandfather who was a milkman in 1931, and explained why I was asking. Four people who seemed to be related wrote back. I invited them to a lunch at the country club on a Saturday, where I told them how grateful I was to Harry Himmel. I gave each of them a copy of my recently published book *Michener and Me*, and in the front of their books I pasted a write-up of the peach pit story. I finished with,

He did the original Heimlich maneuver by having my chest bouncing on his shoulder as he ran down the stairs, and the peach stone blew out. Without a doubt, Harry Himmel saved my life. If he hadn't, [the Michener] book would never have been written. He is truly a hero.

CHAPTER 9

TB or Not TB

Shortly after the miracle of the peach pit, I developed a cough. It was a dry cough I couldn't control. Those around me let me know they found it annoying. My mother took me to the family doctor, who couldn't see anything in my throat or hear anything in my lungs to explain the cough, but he did a patch test for tuberculosis. Children my age, especially in the poorer sections of the city, were catching tuberculosis, so the doctor did a patch test just to be sure I wasn't tubercular.

A week later my arm was somewhat red and swollen, indicating that I might have tuberculosis. My doctor didn't want to take any chances, so he sent me to a sanatorium in Eagleville about fifteen miles from home. The thinking was that within three months either I would develop definitive indications of the disease or my cough would disappear, and I could be considered clear to go home.

I was in the sanatorium for four months before I was cleared to be sent home. It had been a fun time. I had become close friends with the other children, about twelve boys and girls my age. I had always lived among Jewish kids, and my four months in the sanatorium introduced me to kids from many other backgrounds: Irish, Italian, African-American, and Puerto Rican. We enjoyed excellent food, and for recreation we played kissing games.

CHAPTER 10

Working: Hey, Boychick!

"Wanna earn some money?" Calling out to me was the owner of a fruit-and-vegetable store. I was on my way home from Central High School to my tenement apartment in Strawberry Mansion. I always walked along Ridge Avenue, a busy street with many shops and sidewalk stands and a diverse mix of customers looking for bargains to feed their families. It was the Great Depression, so yes, you'd better believe I wanted to earn some money to help my mother, who was raising three sons on her own.

The man was Max Minsky, a rough Jewish immigrant from Russia, whose years of experience as a peddler had helped him achieve success with his store. He had started with a horse and wagon, which he rented on credit, driving his rented horse and wagon to the wholesale market, where he would buy on credit whatever fruits and vegetables were in season. Then he would drive through the streets of Philadelphia, shouting out his wares. Once he had sold everything, he would return the horse and wagon to the stable, pay for the rental, then finish the day at the wholesale market, where he would pay for the produce. He made a good living this way: no capital outlay, no overhead, no advertising, no taxes. His business grew into a thriving produce establishment with a store on Ridge Avenue.

Max Minsky was very intelligent, although that wasn't obvious when you first met him. He was a homely, dumpy, balding man, about forty years old, with a heavy Russian accent that made it difficult to understand what he was saying. But I think he was a genius. He could make complicated computations in his head, and his ideas on selling produce were innovative for his time. He was able to eliminate almost all the work and expense of storing, displaying, and selling his produce.

His store was about thirty feet by sixty feet, a space including a warehouse area and ten tables. The tables were about four feet wide, three feet high, and twenty feet long—rough boards on sawhorses, easily moved.

Each table held wooden peck, quart, and bushel containers of string beans, squashes, potatoes, tomatoes, asparagus, melons—whatever was in season. Prices were clearly posted.

I took Max up on his offer of forty-five cents an hour—good pay in those days. I was to work six hours on Fridays and ten on Saturdays and Sundays. No breaks; we were expected to bring our own food and eat it standing up while we worked.

Each of us boys who worked for Max was responsible for two tables. A customer would approach and point to whatever he or she wanted to buy. We would empty the container—peck, quart, bushel—into a bag, which the customer would take to Max, pay, and leave. We refilled the emptied containers immediately. When the store was busy, we were in motion all day long. Max ran a smooth operation—no weighing, no pricing, no fuss, no muss.

At the end of the day we put the unsold produce back into storage, then lined up in front of Max at the register to receive our pay. We were supposed to get forty-five cents for every hour we worked, but that's not always what happened.

"Moishe, you only get forty cents an hour. I saw you take smoke breaks."

"Haim"—that was me—"you get fifty cents. I saw how you talked customers into buying an extra peck of string beans."

Do you see how I was, even then?

A few years later, while I was home on a visit from the National Farm School, I visited Max. We spoke as friends. I was aware of what I had learned from him: knowledge and practices I later brought to my own businesses. I thanked him for what he had taught me. Here is what I know: You can succeed in business with almost no money, but you must have a sterling reputation to get the credit you need. And you must have a lot of imagination.

CHAPTER 11

··

Working: Robin Hood Dell

In the 1920s the city held free concerts seven nights a week in a pavilion in Fairmount Park. It boasted a fifty-piece orchestra, mostly made up of members of the Philadelphia Orchestra. As many as twenty thousand people came to the concerts, standing as far away as the music carried. On Sunday mornings, there were concerts for children. The concerts were so popular that the city decided to build a new amphitheater to hold ten thousand people.

One day when we came to a part of the park where we used to play, we found a group of men with chain saws, cutting down trees. The cleared land had an interesting slope and lent itself to the big outdoor performing arts venue that became known as the Robin Hood Dell. It became a place where I heard amazing concerts of the Philadelphia Orchestra conducted by Leopold Stokowski. It was also a place where I honed my entrepreneurial skills.

The Robin Hood Dell was usually filled beyond capacity. People would sit on the grass, on benches, on concrete ledges. They were often thirsty and uncomfortable. I made money renting them cushions and selling lemonade during intermission.

When the word got out that Dell was hiring kids, of course some of my friends and I showed up. The deal was that you would pay one dollar up front in the office, for which they gave you a carrier with twelve cups of lemonade to sell for ten cents each, giving us a twenty-cent return on a carrier. But it was important to us to earn as much money as possible, and we figured out a way to do better. We brought cups of our own. Whenever we sold a cup of lemonade, we would put one of our own cups in the empty space and fill it from the remaining cups, eventually leaving only two inches of lemonade for the poor guy after three such exchanges.

The other earning opportunity involved renting cushions. As with the lemonade, we would pay one dollar up front in the office and get five cushions, which we would rent for a quarter apiece. Again, we figured out how to do better: we would bring our own cushions from home. If you had walked into my house on concert nights, you would have found all our cushions gone.

Between the lemonade and the cushions, we made over a dollar for the evening, and when we worked five days, we made five dollars, a lot of money in the Depression.

The best part of the experience was that I got to hear and see great music, opera, and ballet. The other best part was that I learned I could have fun using my imagination to make money.

CHAPTER 12

Working: Blauner's Department Store

Blauner's was a small department store on Ninth and Market Streets in Philadelphia that sold women's and girls' coats. It occupied a good location next to Strawbridge and Clothier and Snellenberg's, two prominent stores. In those days department stores did a big business; the other important ones in Philadelphia were Gimbel's, Lit Brothers, and Wanamaker's in the center of town.

A call went out that Blauner's was hiring high school kids to work evenings and Saturdays. The store was about a mile and a half from Central High. I walked down to apply for a job. A man named Klein was standing on a table. He looked over the fifty or sixty of us who wanted a job.

Klein would select a guy and point to him. "What's your name?"

"Horowitz."

"Come in Friday night at six."

"What's your name?"

"Smith."

Come in Friday night at six."

"What's your name?"

"Gonzales."

"You come in Saturday morning at nine."

He hired everyone but me! I was the last guy in the room, the only one left. He finally noticed me.

"What's your name?"

"Silverman."

"Well, Silverman, I'll tell you. I don't have any jobs left, but if you come in Friday night at six and fold underwear in the ladies' department, I will give you three hours of work."

You will recall that I *like* women's underwear. I came in that Friday night and did a good job, so Klein had me continue to come in every Friday night. Then, with Easter approaching, Blauner's needed more staff because mothers would bring their daughters to outfit them in new coats. Klein came to me. "Tell you what, Silverman. Why don't you come here on Saturday, and I'll put you to work in the girls' coat department."

The coats were beautiful—all kinds of bright colors, orange and yellow and blue. They sold for six dollars or seven dollars or eight dollars or nine dollars. The saleswomen were being paid about forty-nine cents an hour, I think, plus a two- or three-cent commission for every coat they sold. They didn't want to be bothered hanging up coats. That's where we came in, seven stock boys assigned to that Saturday job. We would pick up the coats customers hadn't bought, put them on hangers, and place them on **the racks according to size and style.**

I noticed a showcase off to the side that displayed muffs, mostly made of fake fur, that little girls wore to keep their hands warm when they were dressed up. I thought the muffs were cute and saw it was clever how the muffs had strings that tied around the neck to keep the muffs from getting lost. I observed that customers were looking at the muffs, but no salesladies were paying attention, because the muffs sold for seventy-five cents to a dollar, and the sales staff couldn't be bothered to make a sale for such a low commission.

Guess what? I'd go over to the customers and sell them muffs, and I'd take the sales tags to the salesperson, who would make two cents per sale with absolutely no effort on her part.

When Easter had passed, the manager and head buyer for the department sought me out. As I recall, he said, "Silverman, I noticed what you were doing. More than you were supposed to do. You not only did a good job taking care of your station—I never once saw a coat waiting to go back on the rack—but you also took the time to sell muffs. I am making you head stock boy. Come in every day after school and help me with stock and taking inventory."

This meant I went from three hours a week to thirty, making fifty cents an hour, fifteen dollars a week. Let me tell you, that was real dough. Imagine the joy I felt every week when I gave my paycheck to my mother. I've gotten a lot of checks in my life, many for far more than fifteen dollars, but the one I remember best with the most pride was the first one for fifteen dollars that I gave my mother.

I worked as head stock boy at Blauner's for two years, and the wonderful thing about the job was that in the summertime the department went from kids' coats to women's bathing suits. Here I was, having to go in and out of dressing rooms to remove the bathing suits that didn't fit, and in the meantime I was learning all about female anatomy. With only three brothers, I hadn't seen women undressed. The bathing suit customers looked pretty good to me, and I liked looking.

Anyway, I stayed at Blauner's and made good money until I graduated from Central High, and then it was time to move on to go to the National Farm School.

One ironic aside: do you remember the guy, Klein, who'd stood on the table and hired everyone in the room except me? Newly promoted to assistant buyer, he came to my department to learn how things worked. And there I was, the guy he'd picked last about to teach him how to do inventory and run the department. We laughed about it. He was a good sport.

Blauner's was a great place to work, and I learned a lot there. I learned that people in charge appreciate it when you take responsibility, when you go out of your way to do things that need to be done without being asked, and when you do your job faster than they expect and always do it honestly with integrity. People who want to get ahead in the world should keep this in mind. At least, that is my opinion and experience.

CHAPTER 13

Farm School

This is how a poor seventeen-year-old Jewish boy from Strawberry Mansion went to the Farm School.

I graduated from Central High, the top high school in Philadelphia, with good enough grades to get into a top college, but there was no money to even think about college. Scholarships were few, and student loans didn't yet exist. My pay at Blauner's had risen to twenty-five dollars a week, but all that money had gone toward supporting the family.

A neighbor of mine had a cousin who went to the National Farm School, located in Doylestown, just thirty miles from Strawberry Mansion; and he told me it was free. Sid encouraged me to continue my education; he was working a good job at Gimbel's, earning enough that the family could get by without my contribution.

I sent for information and a catalog. I met the admission requirement: a B average or better in high school and good physical and mental health. Tuition, room, and board were free for the three-year program. Students had to provide only farm shoes and their clothes. You worked, and you took courses, and you could learn to be a farmer or a landscaper. I liked the idea of becoming a landscaper, because I'd spent a lot of time exploring Fairmount Park. So I applied to be one of the twenty-five students to be accepted into the fall semester.

Joseph Krauskopf, an important, internationally know rabbi, had founded the school in 1896. On a visit to Russia, he sought out Leon Tolstoy, whom he questioned about anti-Semitism in Russia. Tolstoy explained that in Russia Jews weren't permitted to own land and were resented for lending money. He advised Krauskopf to return to America to work at putting Jews on the land to become farmers of their own holdings.

Rabbi Krauskopf, whose motto was "Science and Practice," established the National Farm School on seven hundred acres of farmland with fields, orchards, greenhouses, and livestock. The students were to be poor Jewish boys, mostly from Philadelphia.

I remember a very rich, elegantly dressed man in his fancy Center City office interviewing me. He asked me whether I had ever done any hard work. Yes, I had. I told him about unloading a freight car of coal and about the little garden I once had built for myself. He said, "Suppose someone were to tell you to dig a hole and pile the dirt over on one side, and when you were done, they told you to fill it up again. Would you do it?"

I told him I would. Right answer.

"OK, you're in. Now we are going to find someone who will pay the hundred dollars for you to go to school."

The first obstacle to enrolling had been that though the tuition was free, there was a one-hundred-dollar administrative fee. I didn't have one hundred dollars. The school arranged for me to meet a businessman, who after our conversation offered to subsidize me. This man owned a successful fence company on the Main Line outside Philadelphia.

The school taught me to handle hard, physical work.

Although I was studying to be a landscaper, I also had to work on the farm. We milked cows at 6:00 a.m. and twice more each day. We grew and harvested crops. We worked until 6:00 p.m. and until 8:00 p.m. when it was our turn to do the third milking. We had two tractors and about thirty draft horses. I also continued my development as an entrepreneur.

First, I became the school deliveryman for mail and newspapers. The Philadelphia train had a stop at the Farm School. I would meet the early train and take mail and newspapers to the mailroom. I was back in the newspaper business, but this time I was making almost two cents per paper instead of seven-eighths of a cent. I would walk around the dining room, selling papers to students, and then I would do a paper route along two long stretches of Route 202. I cleared about five dollars a week.

Then I added dance lessons to my entrepreneurial activities. For twenty-five cents a lesson, I taught farm boys who had never danced all the basic dances—a half hour, four boys at a time. I realized that if you use your brain and find out what people need, you can make money.

I also made some money by going into Philadelphia to work with a recent Farm School graduate in a small landscape business he'd set up on the street next to Lit Brothers Department Store. I worked there every Saturday and Sunday during the season, selling trees, shrubs, and plants. I would make four or five dollars a day, and I also gained experience in the landscape business. And I started my own landscaping venture, serving customers in the Doylestown area who needed weeding, grass cutting— that kind of work. I hired guys from the Farm School; I charged customers thirty-five cents an hour and paid my guys twenty-five.

Every week I sent money home to my family. I kept some for good times. Saturday night, a big night in Doylestown, was when farmers and their families came to shop. We boys from the Farm School would come into town to check out the farm girls.

I remember the fair that would come to town every year. There were all kinds of rides and stuff to eat, but the best thing was the hootchy-kootchy show. Girls in skimpy clothes danced in front of a tent. A barker would announce that for a quarter we could see girls take off their clothes. A couple of my friends and I paid the quarter, but the girls took off only their tops. For another quarter, the barker told us, we could go into a back room to see a completely naked woman.

In spite of what I'd seen in the changing rooms at Blauner's, I never had seen a completely naked woman. My friends and I paid the extra quarter. Now I knew what all the excitement was about, and I got curious about what it would be like to have sex.

We heard about a whorehouse in Philadelphia. Three of us, all virgins, piled into a car and drove to the section of the city where the whorehouse was supposed to be. We got the exact address from a cabbie. We walked up the steps and rang the bell. A voluptuous woman opened the door and invited us in. We stood in the living room, not having any idea what to do. The woman asked which of us wanted to be first to go upstairs with her. The three of us bolted out the door.

Besides a fascination with female beauty, opportunities for entrepreneurship, commitment to hard work, and the ins and outs of landscaping, one other thing I carried with me from the Farm School was that leadership came easily to me. In my junior year, I was elected president of my class and reelected for my senior year, when I became president of the entire student body.

In 1940 I graduated from the Farm School and started looking for a job. I had a good offer from a large garden market in Columbus, Ohio, paying thirty-five dollars a week plus room and board. When the president of the Farm School heard about the offer, he matched it, asking me to start a farmers' market at the school. I ran the market for two years, and when World War II started, I got a farming deferment along with five students; all the rest were drafted.

Our small team farmed the seven hundred acres, milked a herd of sixty Holsteins, grew all kinds of crops, and spread manure on the fields in winter. We also advertised that local people could pick apples and other fruit from our orchard.

When I drive into the school today, I see rows of trees I planted more than seventy years ago. This always makes me smile, because they are part of my legacy.

Fast-forward.

The Farm School was renamed the Delaware Valley College of Science and Agriculture, and now it granted bachelor's degrees. I was an alumnus, and I had become successful in business, and when I was asked to join the board of trustees, I was happy to accept.

Several years later, when the president retired, I was persuaded to take over the position while they searched for their next president. I committed to four months, which wouldn't interfere with Florida plans with Ann. I immediately met with the student body to tell them what was going on and to offer them access to me, and I reassigned George West, the head of the Business Department, to run the day-to-day operations and improve the existing management situation.

I realized right away that the college had big financial problems. With minimum support from the state and board members, we relied on student tuitions but were having difficulty recruiting students, because we were more expensive than our main competitor, Penn State. We had to raise some money in the short run and come up with a feasible long-term plan.

Here was an institution that owned valuable property. Of the original seven hundred acres, the Farm School had sold or donated land to the Doylestown Hospital, township offices, and sewer authority, but five hundred acres remained. One large parcel was located at a distance from the college; the board agreed we should sell it.

To increase the value of the land, I made a deal with the sewer authority, trading five acres of the property for sewage rights for developers. We held a phone auction during a board meeting. The highest bid was $3 million with 10 percent down. We agreed to give the buyer four months to come up with the balance.

One month before the deadline, the buyer walked away from the deal. We still had his deposit, but the land had dropped $1 million in value. I was able to persuade Joe Conti, the chair of Doylestown Township council, that the parcel would make a great park. The township paid $2 million, we got the money, and the community got a beautiful park.

Now came the bigger challenge. My predecessor realized that the college would never be self-sustaining and had entered into negotiations with Penn State. A merger would double the number of students, raise staff salaries, and do much more. Penn State was eager to proceed. But certain members of our board—egotistical, self-important individuals—didn't want to surrender their board membership for such a merger, and my plan died by one vote.

I suggested that my assistant be named president, and, annoyed with the board's decision not to merge with Penn State, I quit the board and to this day have little to do with the college.

CHAPTER 14

Meeting Ann, Marrying Ann

When I was enjoying my farm deferment and working at the Farm School, I bought a 1930 Ford Coupe with a rumble seat. It wasn't in good shape but well worth the fifteen dollars I paid for it. I had every other weekend off and liked to take it for drives. One Saturday morning I decided to check out the young women at Camp Hofnung in nearby Pipersville.

Camp Hofnung was a camp run by a Jewish organization called Workman's Circle. That was where I had first met Ann when we were kids ten years earlier. Now I remembered that there were many attractive young women counselors, waitresses, and swimming instructors working at the camp, and I set out in my beat-up but trusty Ford to look for girls.

No one seemed to be around; camp hadn't yet opened for the season. But there was a girl working as a book-keeper in the office: Ann Arbeter. A knockout. Beautiful, great smile, beautiful shape. She took my breath away. I waited an hour for her to be free and took her out for lunch: spaghetti and meatballs at the Pipersville Inn, $1.50 each with coffee and dessert.

This was the beginning of a lifelong love affair. I was twenty-one, and she was almost twenty. We would be to-gether for sixty-six years.

I started showing up every night after work. I would eat dinner with the staff, most of whom slept in tents. Ann had her own room on the second floor of one of the houses on the property. I began spending the night with her. At 5:00 a.m. I would sneak along the porch roof, slide down a rainspout, and run to my car. Of course, someone saw me, and rumors immediately spread through the camp. We decided the best thing to do would be to announce we were engaged, which seemed to make it all right for me to spend the nights with Ann.

Now the summer was over, and we needed to tell our parents we were engaged. Ann's mother and father had come to know me when they visited Ann at the camp on weekends. They liked the idea.

My mother did not. She had set her hopes on my mar-rying the daughter of one of her dearest friends, a girl I'd dated briefly in high school but not since. I had no doubts it was Ann I was going to marry. And soon.

We got married in October 1942. Our parents insisted we have a Jewish wedding. That meant we needed a rabbi and a cantor. I asked the rabbi I had known from when

I went to Hebrew School in Pottstown, and Ann asked a cantor she knew, a man with a great voice.

Although her father spent a lot of money to give her a lavish wedding, Ann refused to spend money on a wedding gown; she was married in a rust-colored suit and a matching hat. The rabbi said a few appropriate words, the cantor sang "Be My Love," we said our vows, and I broke the glass. Now we were officially married.

I don't know where Ann's father got the money for a fancy wedding. He was a tailor and didn't make much. He rented a ballroom in the upscale Majestic Hotel on Broad Street. He hired an eight-piece band, arranged for a buffet meal, and invited our families and friends.

Everything was going great until the air raid sirens went off—lights out, drapes closed. Candles were lit, and the band played on as we kept dancing in the dark. When the lights went back on, we saw that almost all the food was gone. People had kept eating in the candlelight—very romantic.

The crazy thing, looking back, is that we didn't take any pictures. I guess nobody had thought about that.

We had only one hundred dollars for a honeymoon. It so happened that one of the instructors at the Farm School was married to a woman whose family owned a bungalow near Lake George. They offered it to us for nothing; all we would need to pay for was a cord of wood, because the cabin had no heat.

We took a train to New York, stayed overnight in an inexpensive hotel, and then took a bus to Lake George. We had dinner and watched bowling before we went to the cabin, where we stayed for five days. It was a beautiful time of year; the leaves had turned, and the days were cool and bright. Our cabin sat in front of a small mountain—perfect for hiking, although we never made it to the top. We tried rowing on the lake, but the wind and waves, and the fact that Ann didn't swim, made us decide against chancing it. We would go to the local grocery store for food and milk. We ate breakfast and lunch at the cabin, having moved the table close to the fire. We were young, in love, and full of joy.

We headed back to work after five days, but the honeymoon never really ended.

We rented a beautiful second-floor apartment above an ice cream store in Danboro, a tiny village near Doylestown. We had two bedrooms, a living room, a bathroom, and a kitchen. It would have been perfect except for one thing: the owners, who lived downstairs, refused to heat our apartment. It got so cold at night that the water in the toilet would freeze.

Our apartment became a second home for classmates on leave from the armed services. We always had one or more overnight guests. The pattern was set for hospitality for the rest of our marriage.

A classmate from the Farm School lent us his Plymouth to use while he was in the army. Another classmate taught Ann how to drive and took her for her driving test.

In the evenings we would go to the movies or hang out next to the movie theater at the Palace of Sweets, where we drank hot chocolate to keep warm. In the spring we rented a house near the Farm School, and a year later we decided on no more renting; we would build our own home.

CHAPTER 15

Military Service

Late in the war the draft board revoked my farming deferment. To tell the truth, I was sick and tired of the hard work of farming and would have begged the army to take me.

On the designated day, I kissed Ann good-bye—big hugs and kisses, tears. I was going into the army, and Ann would be left alone in New Britain (although there were always friends in and out). I walked the two blocks to the station. The conductor said, "Oh, Herman, I see you are going into the army."

"Yup," I said, and that was that. I took the train to Philadelphia and reported to the armory, where they began the induction process.

After an hour I heard over the loudspeaker, "Silverman, report to the office." They were sending me home because somehow my urine sample had been lost. I was to come back the next day. So I got on the train back to New

Britain and walked into my house about noon. I think I scared Ann.

The next day we repeated the tearful good-byes, the hugs and kisses.

The induction process started over. I finally got to see the doctor who would decide whether I was fit to serve in the army. He looked at my feet and saw my freaky toes; I have no metatarsal joint on the fourth toe of both feet next to the pinkie. That probably should have kept me out of the army, because walking is a problem for me, but I was inducted to be assigned to a desk job because I was "unfit for combat."

The doctor's recommendation got lost, and I found myself doing twelve weeks of boot camp at Camp Croft in Spartanburg, South Carolina. Fortunately, on the first day, as we were lined up in uniform with our rifles, the captain asked whether any of us could type. I couldn't, but I raised my hand, and all the other soldiers were marched into one of the hottest days of the year.

The captain explained my duties. I was to type the morning report with a count of how many personnel had reported for duty, how many were in the hospital, and how many were missing. I was also to record staff changes and reassignments, to answer the phone and take messages. And most important, the captain impressed on me that if anyone called to speak to him, I was to say he was on the firing range. Typically, when the soldiers were in the blazing sun, I would be delivering ice water to the officers, who were keeping cool in a tent.

After a few weeks, Ann came down and rented a room for five dollars a week in a small house owned by a woman whose son was in the army. Now the rule was that you couldn't leave the camp during basic training, but I had become friendly with the captain and got up the nerve to ask him for a weekend pass to see my wife. He surprised me by giving me a pass for every night. "Just make sure you're back before roll call every morning." What a break. I wish I could find the captain to thank him for making my life bearable.

Near the end of boot camp, I was tested to see where in the army I would be most effective. I knew I didn't want to be in the signal corps, because that would mean putting myself in the front lines, marching with a heavy radio on my back. So when I was in a cubicle, wearing headphones to work with Morse code, I did everything wrong—dit-dit-dit when they said dot-dot-dot.

The scores came out. "Hey, Silverman, you did great in the radio test, so we are sending you to radio school!" I was assigned to Fort Bragg in Fayetteville, North Carolina, and found myself walking for miles with a radio on my back. After a week of this, the bottoms of my feet split open and bled. I was sent to the hospital. The doctors told me to stay off my feet for several weeks, and I was assigned a teaching job, based on my self-proclaimed "teaching credentials" of having "taught" agriculture at the Farm School. I was to teach new soldiers how to clean radios from the dust and dirt that kept the radios from working. Fortunately, with the war winding down, soon there were no new men to teach, and I was put to work in the officers' mess, cleaning pots and pans from breakfast and lunch, and finishing at 2:00 p.m.

Ann had followed me to Fayetteville and had found a room at the YWCA. And then the war was over, and I was on my way to Fort Dix to be discharged. With my duffel bag full of clothes and my honorable discharge, I hitch-hiked to Philadelphia, where Ann and I had arranged to meet at her mother's house.

Ann got on a train from Fayetteville, arriving in Philadelphia on schedule but having no money for a cab. A taxi pulled up at the station where she was waiting to figure out how she would get to her mother's house. What a lucky coincidence! The cab driver was an old friend and neighbor, a fellow alumnus of the Farm School.

We spent the night in Philadelphia, and the next morning we went back to our house in New Britain. And that was the end of that phase of our lives.

Now what?

My Parents, My Brother Sidney, and Me

Me With My Little Brother Izzy

My Class in Central High School

Courting

The Honeymooners

Never Never Land

Still in Love

My Family at Never Never Land Late 1990's

At the Pool, 1990's

Me, Izzy, and Sid

Our Fiftieth Anniversary

With Jim and Mari Michener at Epcot

Michener Museum Ribbon Cutting With Lina
Buki, Jim Michener, Governor Casey, and Me

Liz, Me, and Friend 1976

"I Do"

Married to Liz

Visiting My Brother-in-law in Santa Fe

At a Fundraiser

Keeping Fit

Still Me, in My Nineties

CHAPTER 16

Building Never Never Land

The house we'd been renting near the Farm School was sold. Ann and I decided we would build our own home—no more renting. But where? And how would we get the money?

We knew we wanted to live close to Doylestown in a house with at least two bedrooms and some land. We had no idea that someday we would need enough land to sell plants in a landscaping business we were starting, to build a large garage with an apartment above it, and eventually to add a swimming pool and a tennis court. Neither did we know that before long we would need at least five bedrooms and a dining room that could accommodate more than twenty people. But we did know what we wanted to build for now.

What a lot of guts I had! With guts but not yet any money I put an ad in the *Doylestown Intelligencer.*

Wanted—3–5 acres within five miles of Doylestown, on a hill, with views, a creek, and woods

Within a few days a man responded to my ad. His lot was only two and a half acres, but otherwise it was just what we wanted—three miles from the center of town and on top of a hill with a view and a stream. Nobody had bought the land, because the hill was too steep to build on unless you were someone who had a lot of imagination. I was able to visualize our house on that hill, and as I said, I did have the guts to go ahead.

We knew we would have to level the hill enough to build a house on it, which meant a lot of earth moving. Leveling the site wouldn't cost us anything, because I'd already bought a bulldozer for my new landscaping business.

We offered the owner $500; he wanted $600, and we agreed. Of course, we needed a mortgage to go forward. I knew I qualified for a GI mortgage, but before we could apply for a mortgage, we needed a building plan.

We found a design we liked in a magazine. The house would be brick with a pitched roof. It would have three bedrooms, three fireplaces, a small kitchen, a dining room, and one bathroom. According to the plans, which we bought, it would cost about $10,000 to build. We applied for a mortgage through a local bank—thirty year at 3 percent of one hundred dollars a month plus taxes. And with the mortgage in hand, we were ready to start building.

With guts, vision, and now almost enough money, we found ways to go ahead. We knew we couldn't afford to buy bricks or hire a bricklayer, so we found a brick-making factory in Easton, about an hour away. It was going out of business and selling its inventory, which included piles of "seconds" in various colors, shapes, and sizes. Ann and I drove our truck to Easton. It took three trips, three loads, but now we had our bricks. We still couldn't afford to pay someone to lay them, so I hired a bricklayer for one day to teach me and four of my landscape-business employees how to do the job.

I'm not known for taking a long time to do a job that can be done well in less time. I decided that the fastest way to lay the bricks would be to lay them in mortar and not bother to do any pointing. Today, if you look at the original house and the three fireplaces, you can tell that professional bricklayers didn't lay the bricks, but the walls did go up quickly.

Now we needed lumber for the roof and inside partitions. Remember, this was just after the war, and lumber was hard to get. There was another piece of good luck—one day when we were laying bricks, a truck from Canada just happened to show up. I gave them a list of what we needed, and a week later we had our lumber.

At this point we knew we needed carpenters, but we didn't know any and had no success in asking around. More good luck: I passed a new house being built nearby that looked as if it would be well made. I approached the carpenters and convinced them that they should work on my house after they finished their regular jobs for the day.

The roof wouldn't be easy. It had all kinds of angles and slopes, but these guys were good. Every evening from five until nine, they worked on our roof. I strung up a light cord so they could work in the dark. These guys were terrific; they finished the roof in five days. I hired a roofer to shingle the roof, and we were good to go.

The plan called for metal windows. I found some in a yard in Philadelphia and picked them up in my truck. I think they added to the beauty of the house.

Next came the interior: inserting partitions for all the rooms, finishing the ceilings, and installing plumbing, electricity, and heat. My men and I were able to do the studding, but those were the days before drywall, and we needed plasterers. I found a crew in Willow Grove. They charged more money than I had budgeted. Then we decided we really needed a second bathroom, and we had to hire outside people to install the plumbing, electricity, and heat. We realized we had to find more money. I arranged for a note for another thousand dollars at 4 percent. With Ann helping to paint the house and my bulldozer moving all the soil, we managed to finish the house in time to move in with our new baby, Jeffra, our firstborn.

This was in the spring of 1948. All the rooms were small. My brother Izzy was living with us while he attended optometry school in Philadelphia. Then, two years later, our second daughter, Leda, was born, and she had to share a tiny bedroom with her sister. Izzy had moved out to serve in the army, but when our third daughter, Binny, was born, we knew we needed a bigger house with more and larger rooms.

By then my business was doing well enough that we could afford a bigger mortgage. We took some risks, pulling out entire walls and propping up the roof. We expanded the existing bedrooms and built on a large master suite with lots of large closets. We tore out the wall to expand the dining room. We ripped out another wall of the living room and created an enclosed space between the bedroom and kitchen wings, giving us a large room that became our TV room. We added two bathrooms. All the while, we were adding exterior walls to support the new construction, and we also built patios and paths, and we landscaped the grounds.

For the new windows we used glass we'd bought from a neighbor, who was a lawyer for a large glassmaking company. They cost very little, because they were "seconds." Instead of putting windows on the long wall of the new dining room, I hired a local artist, Maxie, to paint a mural to my specifications.

Ann gets the credit for the expansion and remodeling. She insisted we needed more and bigger rooms. She loved lots of space and was happy with what we had done with the house. She wanted each of our daughters to have her own room. We thought we were finished with construction, but then our fourth daughter, Jenny, was born, and we added a room for her behind our bedroom.

We also build a two-car garage to store our landscaping equipment, with an apartment above for the couple we employed. Simon and Doris came to work for us around the time Jenny was born, and they made our family's way of life possible. They were with us for twenty years.

Ann had great taste, and it still shows. She could have been a professional decorator. She knew exactly how she wanted to furnish the house, and our first furniture still remains in it. I have given the house to my four daughters; they and their families and friends use it for parties, holidays, special occasions, and a place to go to in the country. It still looks much as it did when we finished building it.

We named our home Never Never Land, because both of us and our children love the story of Peter Pan. Some people have suggested that Ann and I are like Wendy and Peter Pan and that I never will grow up.

One point I want to make is that no architect was ever involved in the house and garage we built. We used our imaginations, ingenuity, and good sense; and our house worked just as we thought and hoped it would. One of my granddaughters is an architect. She says it's obvious that we built the house without the help of an architect, but she gave the greatest praise when she said, "It works."

The other point I want to make is that building the house was part of the same process as building our family. Ann and I figured out for ourselves how to proceed as we went. We created a spacious, well-built, comfortable house, where our children's friends as well as ours would feel welcome, where they could feel confident and secure.

What we expected of our children and later our grand-children was that they would build on the solid foundations of their upbringing. We expected their lives to reflect and pass along the hospitality, generosity, hospitality, humanitarianism, and other values they learned while growing up in Never Never Land.

CHAPTER 17

....

Watch Us Grow!

The war was over. Ann and I were married. I was back at work at the Farm School, and Ann was keeping the books for a small grocery store. We had very little money.

I was determined to go into business for myself. Remember, it was 1946, just after the war, and equipment was hard to find—no front-end loaders, no backhoes. And I didn't have the money to buy a lot of equipment anyway. But I had my Farm School education in landscaping and saw that there would be little competition.

What I had to have right away was a truck. The army had hundreds of surplus trucks and jeeps stored in the field of a big farm in Reading. For $500 and an honorable discharge, you could buy any vehicle you wanted. I had the honorable discharge but not the $500. So I did the obvious thing and applied for a loan at a local bank.

I told the banker I needed $500 to start my business. The banker informed me that I had no credit, and therefore they wouldn't lend me the money. "Sorry, we can't help you."

Now, this is the part of the story I like best. When I walked out of the bank, I shook my fist at it and swore that someday I would own the bank. In 1980 I bought the building, and I still own it.

But what to do? I needed a truck, and I needed $500 to buy it. I turned to a friend at the Farm School, now the dean, and borrowed the money from him. I drove right out to Reading and came home with a one-ton truck. So finally I was in business.

I put a big sign on my truck: "Sylvan Landscape Service, Watch Us Grow."

On weekends I would drive around the areas where new housing was being built and people were moving in, where the yards were bare and ugly. I would make sketches of their houses, showing my proposed plantings, shrubs, and trees; and then I knocked on the door.

"I just made a sketch of your home, and I'd like to landscape it. May I come in and show you how it would look?" Most homeowners were an easy sell. I would tell them, "It's gonna cost you thirty bucks," and they usually bought my idea. I could get five to ten new customers this way every weekend.

And then I'd drive my truck to a local nursery, where I would dig up plants, and during the week I would plant them for my customers. Then I would collect my money, pay the nursery what I owed, building up credit with them. (Remember Max Minsky and his vegetable wagon in Strawberry Mansion? I obviously did.) Then I would get some new customers.

It took only a couple of months for the business to take off. Within a year I bought a beat-up bulldozer, paying it off in monthly installments, and I was even able to hire a couple of guys, paying them well.

My reputation as a landscaper grew with my business. As I said, there wasn't much competition, and there was a need for my services, mostly to landscape the inexpensive houses in these developments that were springing up all around Doylestown.

And then in April I got a call from Oscar Hammerstein's manager, asking me to come to the Hammerstein house. A trellis covered with wisteria vines had collapsed. I attached a roll of turkey wire to the chimney, allowed it to unroll to the ground, and attached the vines. Hammerstein came out to say hello and to thank me for the job. The manager then asked me, while I was there, whether I could look at a maple tree that lost its leaves by June every year. This tree was in the center of a circular driveway and had become an eyesore.

I was confident that I could save the tree. I punched maybe fifty holes in the ground all around the outside of what they call drip lines, where the feeding roots are, about ten feet from the trunk. Then I poured fertilizer in all the holes, got a soaker hose, and laid it down to soak the fertilizer, keeping the holes filled with water day and night for two days.

After that the tree never lost another leaf before autumn. Hammerstein decided I was a miracle worker. He hired me to do more landscaping for him, and before I knew it, I was doing a lot of landscaping for celebrities who had bought farms in Bucks County, people like Budd Schulberg, Pearl Buck, and Moss Hart.

While I was growing my business, I was also building my home. It was in the context of home and my landscaping business that a few years later I ended up creating an industry. It all began when Ann asked me to build her a swimming pool...

CHAPTER 18

Starting an Industry with Sylvan Pools

We had a neighbor, a mason who did concrete work, who'd built a pond in his backyard. When Ann saw it, she asked me to build her a swimming pool. I didn't have a mason working with me, and I had no idea about how to build a swimming pool; after all, I was a landscaper and landscape designer. But I asked myself, How hard could it be? You dig a hole, you pour in cement for the floor and walls, you fill it with water, and you have a swimming pool.

So that's what we did. We dug a hole in our backyard and lined the bottom and sides with steel turkey wire. (I love turkey wire—you will recall that it's what I used to fix Hammerstein's wisteria problem.) I rented a hand-operated concrete mixer; bought some sand, stone, and cement; mixed it all up; and poured it into the hole.

Up until that time, pools were expensive. They were made with wood forms. The floor was separate from the walls. The construction took a long time, with much higher labor costs, and the pools weren't resistant to freezing weather.

I didn't realize right away how novel and brilliant my technique was. There were no seams to leak, and because of its pear-like bowl shape, when the water froze in the winter, the ice would just slide up the walls. The slant of the walls and the pear shape made the pools very strong, reducing the pressure from the dirt surrounding them, which would tend to press them inward. Later an engineer told me this is called the "angle of repose."

When we poured the cement, we added eyebolts every three feet near the tops of the walls and put in half-inch ropes to give swimmers something to hold on to. We bought a sliding board and ladder from a company we found on Long Island. We filled the pool, we added chlorine to keep the water clean, and we vacuumed the dirt that settled on the bottom.

Soon our children, their friends, and our friends were swimming happily in our pool. It didn't leak. It was perfect. I realized I had successfully created a fast and cheap way of building a great pool.

That fall I mentioned our pool to Hammerstein. He came to see it and liked what he saw. Early on New Year's Eve, he summoned me to his house, because he'd decided he couldn't wait to discuss putting a pool on his property. Ann and I had plans for the evening, but I agreed to meet with him, and, knowing he had a liking for fruit, I quickly sketched a pear-shaped pool to show him. He signed a contract on the spot. And soon I had calls to build pools for several celebrities in Bucks County.

As word got out, we built more and more pools until it was clear that we needed to get out of the landscaping business and concentrate on building pools. We changed the company name to Sylvan Pools. Our logo, drawn by a friend of mine, showed a cartoon king diving into a pool with the slogan "Live Like a King."

We constantly improved our product with steeper walls and by incorporating tiles, filters, and plumbing. Soon we were recognized as the leader in the field. Every year at the National Swimming Pool Institute Convention, there were contests for the best pools from the previous year. We won almost all of them.

The business exploded. Doylestown became the place to look when considering a pool. *Fortune Magazine* published a book, *One Hundred Successful Small Businesses*, that included Sylvan Pools, which in truth was no longer all that small. *Fortune Magazine* also published a story about me, "The Cheap Swimming Pool Man," and proclaimed that I had started pool building as an industry.

We also got a spread in *Life* magazine after I had built a pool for one of the editors, who decided to do a story on pools and pool toys. It was March. I heated up our pool and recruited my daughters and five of their friends. The photographer set up on the roof of the dining room and spent half a day taking pictures of my girls and their friends in the pool.

The two-page spread came out in May. The caption along the bottom read, "Sylvan Pool 20' x 40' $4,000." The response was huge, and I realized I needed two things: a professional to handle publicity and a highly visible pool store. I hired a publicist to send out press releases with instructions to get stories about Sylvan Pools into magazines and newspapers, including coverage of the commercial pools we were now building in various towns and cities. One of our pools was featured on the cover of *House Beautiful*.

I bought ten acres on the main highway just outside Doylestown, just a mile from our house. There I built a pool store and offices. On the roof of the building I put the figure of a beautiful young woman standing on a diving board. You could see it for miles.

We advertised on train platforms and highway billboards. The commercial pools we built for cities and country clubs usually got a lot of press in their towns, and they always mentioned Sylvan Pools as the pool builder. We also got publicity from the Instant Swim Pool I invented, an aluminum, aboveground pool two men could build in one day. Instant pools sold to municipalities all over the country, forty-five in Baltimore alone, and four big ones in Washington, DC.

And before long Sylvan Pools became the largest pool company in the United States.

My pool design continues to be used in residential settings, hotels, motels, country clubs, the army and navy, camps, and cities.

Once in a while I meet someone who tells me I built a pool for his or her parents or grandparents. I always ask, "Does it still hold water?"

He or she always answers, "Yes."

And then I tell him or her, "They got one of the lucky ones."

CHAPTER 19

Challenges, Ingenuity, and Stories of Running Sylvan Pools

1. The company was growing, but there was a time one December when we had to face the reality that we had lost a lot of money. We couldn't afford to pay our suppliers—concrete people, plumbers, lumber companies, steel companies, and others. We owed more than $200,000 to about twenty creditors.

To get out of debt, we had to build pools, lots of pools. Without the suppliers, we wouldn't be able to build more pools. So I contacted every one of our suppliers and invited them to lunch at Doylestown's best restaurant. They didn't expect my pitch.

"Now look, I owe money to each of you in this room. All of you will be paid dollar for dollar. But I want you to help me. I want each of you to kick in a percentage of the money

I owe you. I will put out three to four million inserts in the Sunday papers, the *Washington Post*, the *Baltimore Sun*, the *Newark Star Ledger*, the *Philadelphia Inquirer*, and the *New York Times*. This will bring in so much business that everyone will get paid, but I need you people to help me."

They agreed, and we had the money for my big advertising idea, not that we had any money to hire advertising people. I went to the *Inquirer* and asked their advertising department to lay out the supplement for me. They produced an eight-page supplement. On one page we listed all the suppliers, thanking them for their contributions. We used lots of color and displayed all the types and shapes of pools we offered with the prices of each. The *Inquirer* ran off four million copies and shipped them to the various newspapers. They charged me only for the printing.

The supplements arrived in people's Sunday papers early that April, and the whole swimming pool industry came back to life. People started talking about pools they knew only from the pictures, and our business was flourishing again. We jacked up our prices and paid off all our suppliers. What's more, we gave the public the impression that we were the number-one pool company to do business with.

To show my appreciation to the people at the *Inquirer*, I invited them to dinner. Apparently the customer ordinarily doesn't invite them to dinner, but rather they invite the customer. We had a grand time, and after that they always made sure that our ads had the best placement in their Sunday magazine section.

2. Sometime in the 1980s the northeastern states from New England to Maryland experienced a severe drought. The pool industry was hit hard. The governor of Pennsylvania declared a water emergency, limiting water use to what was needed for health and home. He urged people to take quick showers, to put bricks in the toilet tanks to reduce the amount of water needed to flush; he even asked everyone to flush only when absolutely necessary. Nobody was permitted to water his or her lawns or wash his or her cars and trucks—and worst of all for Sylvan Pools, nobody was allowed to fill his or her pool.

We were just coming out of a hard winter. Sylvan Pools had a big backlog of orders, and we needed the money the pools would provide. Not being able to build and fill pools would create a serious problem, not just for us, but for all the pool builders.

I figured out how we could solve the problem and told the governor's aide, whom I knew well from sitting next to him at Pennsylvania Housing Finance Agency board meetings, that I needed to see the governor about drought restrictions. He invited me to Harrisburg the next day.

When I arrived at the governor's office, I was told that he had an emergency and was about to go to the local airport to fly to Erie. I let him know it was urgent that I talk with him, so I got into his car with him and explained my idea to save the pool industry.

I knew fire companies were worried about having enough water to put out fires. Water levels throughout the East were low, and without adequate water, fires could be catastrophic. My idea was to have all the Pennsylvania pool companies as well as present and future owners of pools sign an agreement with the fire companies, allowing them to use the water in their pools to fight fires.

The governor thought this was a good idea. He said, "Do it," and I immediately called a meeting of all the pool companies. We met in a local hotel. I told them what I had done, and I passed out agreements for them to sign and take to their local fire companies.

At the next pool convention, I received an award for "saving the pool industry."

3. When I was first building pools and still doing landscaping around 1955, I had a call from a Mr. G, who wanted some landscaping done and a pool installed in a home he'd just bought on Pineville Road. Formerly owned by a prominent Philadelphia politician, it was a premium piece of real estate, with a farm and a gorgeous Bucks County stone house. Mr. G was impressive to look at, too, a handsome man of about sixty, immaculately dressed, even on a Sunday morning in the country, his name embroidered on his shirt pocket, his shirt, slacks, and shoes smacking of wealth.

We bonded right away. I liked the way he would smile slightly when he talked, as if he were enjoying our meeting.

His Brooklyn accent was incongruous, but I thought nothing of it.

We were in the den, chitchatting before discussing business, when a knockout of a woman appeared. Mr. G. introduced her as Daisy. No title, just Daisy. I wondered, Was she his wife? Sister? Girlfriend? It soon became clear that I was to work with Daisy, that she was his girlfriend, that Mr. G had to go to work every day in his chauffeured car, and that I should do whatever Daisy wanted.

As it happened, there already was a pool on the property, one I had built for the previous owner, and Mr. G intended to keep using it. But Daisy needed her own pool, because she didn't like cold water. I was to build a pool for her, keeping the water above 87 degrees. I pointed out that this would require an extralarge pool heater. "No problem," Mr. G said. "Whatever Daisy wants."

Daisy also had some ideas for the landscaping that had to be done to keep her happy. The property did need a lot of lawn work and plantings around the house, but Daisy didn't like the fence at the end of the property, because, she said, it was too flat and boring. Before planting the red roses she absolutely had to have, she wanted me to make the land look hilly and to install an appropriately wavy fence. We would have to bring in lots of topsoil and redig all the fences. It would be a huge job.

Mr. G had one request: he wanted an orchard with pears and apples so he could eat straight from his own trees.

One more thing: Daisy planned to throw a big party for Mr. G's sixtieth birthday. She walked me privately to the center of the lawn, where there was a beautiful sycamore tree. She instructed me to build a putting green there, with a sign saying she had made it as a birthday present for Mr. G.

Mr. G finally asked me for an estimate. I told him I could quote him a price for the pool, but the rest of the work would be billed for cost of labor and materials. He asked for a week to think it over. He decided to go ahead.

Every Saturday I would give him a bill for the week's work. He would look at the bill to see whether it was OK, pay me with one-hundred-dollar bills he had in his pocket, and tell me to continue for the following week. For the pool he gave me a check for the agreed-upon price, but for everything else, the same routine, I'd show up on Saturday morning, he'd look at the bill showing what work I had done, and he would pay me in one-hundred-dollar bills.

This went on for two months. Then one morning I picked up the paper, and there was a picture of Mr. G— only the article gave his name as that of the head of the New Jersey Mafia and stated that he'd been called to appear before the Kefauver Commission.

I immediately went to his house. Empty. Nothing left but a stove and three window air conditioners. Also gone was the $2,000 I would have collected for the week's work.

A few months later on a cold winter day, I got a call from Daisy. She wanted to know how much of the cash

Mr. G had given me had been deposited in the bank. Most of it, I told her. The she asked me how much Mr. G still owed me, and I told her. Another two months went by, and she called me again. She told me to meet her at a hotel in Center City at 4:00 p.m. the next day. So I drove to Philadelphia and found her in the lobby.

The glamor girl was gone; Daisy was dressed unobtrusively in a woolen coat and large hat that hid her face. We retreated to a secluded corner of the lobby. She counted out $2,000 in one-hundred-dollar bills. I was wearing a long winter overcoat, and I stuffed the money into my pocket. I thanked her, wished her well, and left.

I never heard from either of them again.

4. In the late 1960s, in the wake of the assassination of Dr. Martin Luther King Jr., there was a lot of unrest in poor, inner-city neighborhoods. I had an idea that public swimming pools would be beneficial in those neighborhoods. If I could build a lot of aboveground pools that could be put up quickly and taken down quickly, and that were easy to clean and safe, I could give the kids in these neighborhoods something to do and a chance to cool off.

I asked an engineer on staff to design a pool using aluminum panels, with a fence and walkways. We bought the panels in twelve-foot lengths from a plant in Camden and cut them in three to use for pool walls. We contracted with another company to make liners to fit inside the pool structure and to hold the water. We put the prototype, with its walkway, fence, and filters, on the lawn next to the entrance to our pool store in Doylestown.

Now to sell them. We put stories in parks and recreation publications and sent literature to all the town park departments in the area. We invited people to see the sample pool we had set up in Cherry Hill, New Jersey. About twenty people came, and the orders started right away.

The pools ran from $4,500 to $10,000, depending on size, and could be built anywhere where there was a flat, even surface. The city of Baltimore ordered forty-five of the big pools, a huge $400,000 order. We had to make the panels quickly. I bought a small storage building half a mile from our office, where I set up an assembly line to cut and package the aluminum panels and where I could store the plastic liners and filters. We set up four crews of three men each who put up forty pools in two weeks. We got a lot of publicity, and Baltimore had its swimming pools.

The head of the Baltimore Parks Department had become a good friend. It was he who called me on the Fourth of July. "Herman, one of your pools split open. Some kids on the walkway landed on the ground. The mayor is very worried. He thinks you may have to take the pools out. He wants a meeting on Monday morning at eleven to decide what to do."

I wrote a check for $400,000, payable to the city of Baltimore, which as you might have guessed wouldn't have cleared our bank account. But remember, I always dealt with problems by relying on imagination and guts.

The engineer and I met on the New Jersey Turnpike at 7:00 a.m. Monday morning and got to Baltimore in time to look at the defective pool before the meeting. We found that a corner bolt holding one end of the pool to a side panel had broken. Our demo pools had stood on grass. This pool had been set up on a tennis court, which couldn't absorb the vibrations from the pool in use. My engineer told me he could fix the problem with a half-inch cable for reinforcement.

On the way into the meeting, I told the head of the Parks Department that I had a check with me for $400,000, the full cost of the forty pools, and was prepared to remove the pools. I realized the mayor probably must have been feeling very anxious and wanted to lower his anxiety level. My friend, the head of the Parks Department, announced at the beginning of the meeting that I was prepared to pay for and remove the pools.

The mayor asked whether we had a lawyer with us. I told him we didn't need a lawyer, that we knew exactly what the problem was, and that if he would close the pools for one week, we could fix it.

The mayor asked the building inspector for his opinion. The building inspector asked us what we would do and approved of the plan. Lucky for us, it worked, we made a nice profit, and we got a contract to dismantle and store the pools at the end of the season.

5. I have been searching for the right word to describe what happened with my top executives at Sylvan Pools.

Perfidy? Nefarious scheming? Let's just say these men behaved badly and could have destroyed the business.

About twenty years after we founded the business, the vice-president of Anthony Pools contacted us and made us a good offer to buy Sylvan Pools. Anthony Pools was big in the West and wanted to be a presence in the East. My brother and partner, Ira, and I thought about it, decided we could do better as we were, and turned down the offer.

Our four vice-presidents of sales, construction, finance, and retail weren't pleased with our decision. With Ira and me out of the picture, they were sure Anthony would keep them on at higher salaries. They also expected to get stock from Anthony, a company trading on the stock exchange. Ira and I ran the company as a partnership, so we had no stock to give out.

Late one evening, not long after I had turned down the Anthony offer, I got a call at home from the head of our Engineering Department. He was working late, unbeknown to the vice-presidents who were setting up their scheme in the next room. He'd overheard them developing a scheme by deliberately losing sales and increasing the costs of construction. The plan was to find ways to reduce Sylvan Pools' profits to soften Ira and me up and make us more receptive to Anthony's offer. The engineer assured me that he'd heard their conversation clearly and that they were dead serious about their plan.

Ira and I were shocked, bewildered, horrified. We decided right away that all four of the traitors would have to go. But how were we to go about firing these no-good bums? Individually or all together? We were in no mood for a confrontation. We decided to call them in for an early-morning meeting. Before they arrived, we had their offices emptied and all the furniture piled in front of their doors. They got the message, and we avoided any confrontations or altercations.

Fortunately, we had good people we could promote to the vice-presidencies. The company carried on without skipping a beat.

What became of the four vice-presidents we fired? The sales manager was out of work for a long time but eventually got a job selling paper products. The finance manager sold jewelry in a small, nondescript store in Princeton. The construction manager did all right; he became a partner in a company building apartment houses. I don't know what happened to the retail vice-president.

I never carry a grudge. When I think about what happened, I have to laugh. All I feel is amusement.

On the other hand, Ann was furious.

6. Now, this one isn't going to be a cheerful or amusing piece. Property damage and accidents happen when you build pools for people. Lawsuits follow. Little did I imagine that being in the swimming pool business would result in having to deal with lawyers in every one of the states where we operated.

Building a pool in a backyard is a big construction job. The customer never anticipates how much of his or her property will be dug up with dirt piled, rocks blasted, sidewalks broken up by the big trucks, and occasionally basement walls in the house damaged so they cave in. For most of these problems, we hired local lawyers, who were able to settle most of these cases before they came to court.

Swimming pools can be dangerous when people using them forget common sense or don't pay attention. When people get hurt doing crazy things, they most likely sue. Our insurance company handled most of the claims for serious injuries, which often took a year or more to come to trial, and then we lost almost all the cases because of the "Failure to Warn" law. This law required that each and every piece of equipment, machinery, or material that might cause harm be labeled with a permanent stamp or sign saying that misuse of the product could cause injury.

Common sense and fairness didn't prevail in many of these cases. One lawsuit was regarding a pool I had built twenty years earlier; it had a slide on it, and the house had just been sold. The new owner filled in the pool to build an extension on the house and sold the slide at a yard sale. The person who bought it installed it in the shallow end of his pool, two feet deep instead of the requisite four-foot minimum.

A young girl went down the slide, was injured, and ended up paralyzed. The girl's parents sued the slide company and Sylvan Pools. Although the insurance company did its best to establish that we had nothing to do with the incident, the jury awarded the family $1 million; we had to pay 20 percent of the award. The slide company went belly-up, and we had to pay the full amount. The judge cited "Failure to Warn." The insurance company paid the million dollars.

In another case we built a pool for a family in Philadelphia—standard size, two to four feet deep in the shallow end. On one hot Sunday the family threw a pool party. Lots of beer was consumed. The men decided to see who could dive the farthest. One man stood in the shallow end and spread his legs apart, challenging the diver to dive all the way across the pool and between his legs. The owner of the pool went first. He took a running start and made it to the shallow end between his friend's legs, but he hit his head on the bottom of the pool. He was paralyzed. The insurance company settled for several million dollars. The judge instructed the jury about the "Failure to Warn" law; he said we were supposed to have signs on the pool to warn against diving in the shallow end.

Yet another lawsuit was from a pool we had built for a swim club. On one Sunday a man wanted to have fun with his young son in the diving pool. He had his son sit on the edge of the pool, while he jumped off the diving board to "water bomb" his son. On his second dive, he hit the pool wall and was seriously injured. He sued the club for allowing him to jump into the pool from the diving board, and he sued Sylvan Pools for providing a diving board with too much spring. The jury found for the father. The insurance company split the award with the swim club.

We didn't lose every suit against us. Here is one we actually won. On a dare, a drunken guest at a pool party jumped into one of our pools out of a second-story window and broke both of his legs. The judge threw out the case.

The most serious and deeply tragic incident happened at a motel pool we'd built in New Jersey. One Sunday I got a call from the municipal police department, informing me that five people had just been electrocuted in the pool. A little boy had dived into the pool and hadn't come back up; four men had dived in to save him, and all five were dead. I immediately called my electrician and a New York attorney, and an hour later we met at the pool. The electrician verified that there was a lethal charge of electricity in the water.

How could this be? In the bathhouse next to the pool, our electrician found that the circuit breakers the motel electrician had connected to the pool lights had later also been connected to the motel entrance and exit signs. He tested the breakers and found the problem. A truck belonging to the construction crew working on the property had knocked over the "Enter" sign, shorting out the wiring, which caused the electricity to travel back under a deck and into the water.

This clearly was not our fault, but it did happen in one of our pools. My brother and partner, Ira, worked with the insurance company to prove we had no responsibility for this tragedy. Ira hired a professor of electrical engineering at Rutgers to make the argument for us, and eventually we were excused from the lawsuits. But we wanted to make sure it would never happen again. We hired the professor to work with the electrician and the underwriter to design a system that would ground every pool. Each pool would have to ground all metal ladders, pool lights, and diving stands to pass underwriting standards before the concrete was poured.

At the next national meeting of swimming pool manufacturers, Sylvan Pools was recognized for this safety initiative.

CHAPTER 20

Aqua Club and the Fountainhead, a Terrific Idea That Wasn't

What made me think I could make big money by owning a swim club with a restaurant and nightclub?

The idea came to me in 1960. We had been building pools for swim clubs, one of them for a New Hope resident who'd ordered a pool for his Main Line development. Too bad for this man; he went bankrupt with the pool completed but not fully paid for. The judge awarded me the pool as my share in the assets. I got five acres of valuable ground as part of the deal and proceeded to do the necessary landscaping.

Now I owned a large Sylvan commercial pool. The development had about a thousand homes. I needed five hundred memberships at $300 each to make an acceptable profit. I was able to hire a good staff; many of the lifeguards were teachers, and we also hired a couple to run the kiddie pool. Soon we had five hundred members and a good thing going, and I needed to spend only two or three hours a week at the club. Three years later I accepted a good offer from the YMCA, and I was happy to sell it.

Building a swim club in Central Bucks County seemed like a no-brainer. My friend Jim Michener, who was staying with us, was interested in investing. I took him on as a partner in what we were calling the Aqua Club. Jim invested $30,000 to become a 30 percent partner.

We bought twenty acres of good, flat land just south of New Hope on Route 202 and began building an L-shaped pool large enough to accommodate five hundred families. Jim persuaded me to hire a friend of his, "Vit," who showed up with his wife and three children and no means of support; so of course I hired him. He'd been fired from a government job on Guam after a general identified him as a communist, which he wasn't; he was just a very liberal guy. We built the pool and soon filled the club with five hundred members. Ann and our daughters went to the club every day. Vit had helped build the club, and now he ran it for us.

We had a good thing going. We really did.

Now, here is the terrific idea that wasn't. It seemed like a terrific idea to build a smaller pool and restaurant for private parties as well as a nightclub. So we did. We called it the Fountainhead. Those were the days when everybody was talking about Ayn Rand's best seller. Of course, had we read the book ourselves, we never would have chosen to name our club the Fountainhead, because Ayn Rand represented values and a world view Ann and I rejected. Maybe that was part of the jinx.

The club lost money right away. For one thing I didn't know I should have kept closer tabs on the bartenders and what they did and didn't deposit in the till. Three years later, we owed banks and suppliers about $100,000, and Jim refused to invest any more money. We decided to sell.

Our accountant advised us to file for bankruptcy, but I was determined to pay our debts in full. We held a Monday-morning meeting to consider the disaster and what we were going to do. Thirty years later Jim alluded to our meeting in a letter. He quoted himself as saying, "Herman, you and I cannot afford to go into bankruptcy. It is against the grain of our personal lives. I'm convinced that you are destined to be an important man in this community and I expect to keep my typewriter working. Let's pay off the debts right now, get this damned thing behind us, and get on with our lives. There are good years ahead."

Jim was right.

We were able to borrow enough money, and we held an auction to pay off our creditors. All of them were made whole; all of them were paid every cent we owed them. Still, we lost a bundle. Eventually I bought Jim out of the partnership, promising him $10,000 a year for six years, doubling his initial investment. Jim accepted my generous offer, and I gave his share of the partnership to my brother Ira. Years later Jim's wife, Mari, told me he should have held on to his 30 percent share of Sylvan Pools as our business grew and thrived.

Vit had returned to Guam by then, as Jim had used his influence to clear Vit's name and have his security clearance restored.

The big lesson I learned was that I should stick with what I knew I was good at.

CHAPTER 21

Selling Sylvan Pools and Then What?

Let the good times roll! It was the sixties. Businesses were flourishing, new corporations were forming, big companies were swallowing up smaller companies, and Ira and I were watching other people bank big bucks. "Why were we not getting part of the action?" we asked. We had built the company from my initially borrowed $500 to what was probably the largest swimming pool company in the country.

Ira and I started talking about how we might take advantage of our success and the prosperity of the times and get some serious money we could keep. Until then we were taking small salaries, using the cash we'd generated to grow the company. Here was our thinking: let's put the company on the stock market, sell shares, and use some of the money to continue to build the the company and some for ourselves. We would be rich. We, two poor Jewish boys from Strawberry Mansion, would be rich, very rich!

We would have a secure nest egg if the pool business went bad, which we knew it could if the economy went bad, if people began to worry about money, or if cold and rainy weather became the norm.

It seemed like a brilliant plan; only we had no idea how to get listed on the stock exchange. Our accountant knew someone at Merrill Lynch who gave us the name of their vice-president in charge of mergers and acquisitions. We made an appointment in New York to meet with this guy and start the process of getting Sylvan listed on the big board. We took our accountant along to help with the numbers and brought our financial reports; we expected the Merrill Lynch VP to be impressed.

Brooks Brothers suit, buttoned-down shirt, college tie, vest—he was very Waspy, working for a Waspy company. He studied our financial statements and asked a lot of questions about our plans for the future.

At the end of two hours, he summarily blew us off. He said we weren't big enough to be listed on the stock market, but perhaps a big, larger company already on the stock exchange could acquire us.

Somebody was a blabbermouth. We don't know who started the rumors, but word soon got out that Sylvan Pools was "in play," to use a stockbroker term. The buzzword those days was *synergy*, meaning that if you put one company worth "1" with another company worth "1," you got a combined value of "3." It didn't take long for three companies to contact us, all of them good, solid, and listed on the stock exchange.

After looking at our financials, the three companies were interested enough to arrange a meeting of their representatives with Ira and me. They wanted to look us over, to check out our real estate holdings, to meet some of the people who worked for us, and to look at our equipment and inventory. Most importantly, they wanted to get to know Ira and me.

Remember what we are talking about—our company merging into their company. We would receive cash and stock, and we would get a management contract to work for them. We would no longer own our company; they would own all the real estate and equipment. They would be our boss. We would receive a salary and have additional income from owning their stock and the profit it produced.

After several months of meetings and visits, we started to get proposals to merge, most of which were a combination of stock and cash, with cash being a small part and stock being a big part. In effect they were asking us to gamble that their company was already worth a lot of money and would grow and that we would benefit from their success. We did believe this was possible, but we were uneasy. All this was new to us. We realized that we'd better educate ourselves—and fast.

We did some research and found out about an organization in New York that gave classes on various business subjects. Ira and I signed up for a one-week class on mergers and acquisitions. The most important thing we got out of the course was learning that what we were considering, merging our company with another, was very, very risky. Not a job for amateurs.

After the class ended, we approached the instructor, an economist who had impressed us with his expertise in mergers and acquisitions, and asked him whether we could hire him to help us reach a decision as to which company we should merge with. He requested the names of the three interested companies, copies of their proposals, and our financial statements for three years. Once he had a chance to look things over, he would call us with his advice.

Less than a month later, he called to say he was ready to come to Doylestown and give his opinion. We picked him up at the Trenton train station at 10:00 a.m. He informed us that he was an Orthodox Jew and had to be home before sundown, which meant he had to leave us by 3:00 p.m., so we didn't spend a lot of time on chitchat. He opened our meeting by asking us why we were merging the company. We told him we wanted a nest egg and some security, because the pool business had ups and downs and because we sometimes worried about our future finances.

He responded loud and clear. "Stocks are not a nest egg; only cash is a nest egg."

Our reply was, "Look at all the stock they are offering. How far down could it go?"

His answer, still loud and clear: "Zero."

We spent the next few hours going over the financial value of each of the three companies. When we finished, we asked him which company we should go with, and he answered, "The one who gives you the most cash. Tell your lawyers to negotiate with each of them. Tell them how much cash you want, and any stock you get is icing on the cake."

I questioned him further. "If we take stock, we could defer income taxes because we won't be taxed until we sell the stock, but if we take cash, we will be hit with a big income tax."

He replied, "Pay the taxes. Then you have your nest egg free to do as you please."

We contacted our lawyer, who also happened to be an accountant; even though he was only forty, he was an experienced negotiator and a very tenacious guy. He started negotiating with the three companies and finally got it down to one, the one who agreed to our cash demands. He started to negotiate on the amount of stock we would get.

I personally was OK with the stock the companies offered, but he wasn't. I don't like indecision; I get impatient. I'd say, "Make the deal," and he'd say he could get more. We finally did get a lot of stock, more than we expected. The deal was closed in New York in December 1969, and after all our respective hands were shaken, my new boss, president of the company that bought us, said, "Don't ever send your lawyer around again. He's too tough."

At the closing I received a very large check, and my lawyer advised me to find a bank, open up a savings account, and deposit it immediately. He wanted me to start collecting interest on the large amount. I was advised to start investing in the stock market, which I never did. The first thing I did was pay off my loans at the bank, loans I'd needed to live on while I was drawing such a small salary. I gave 20 percent to my wife, which she immediately gave to a Merrill Lynch agent, who invested in Fannie Mae bonds, a good idea at that time. I also set up a trust for my four daughters so they would have financial security and a guarantee of a comfortable life.

Now we were no longer the bosses, but Ira and I still ran Sylvan Pools with all the same employees. The only things that really changed were that Ira and I were well paid with benefits and that we sent the company profits to a bank in Cincinnati. The deal with the company required us to stay for five years. I stayed another five; he stayed another ten.

As for our many shares of stock, five years after we were acquired, the country fell into recession. Banks and businesses were failing or going bankrupt, and the company that had bought us was one of them. The stock I had bought at twenty-seven dollars a share fell to three dollars a share. We were glad we had negotiated for mostly cash. For the company to get out of bankruptcy, it had to put together a plan with the banks and creditors, and it doubled the stock we owned, which shot up to six dollars and eventually went up to where it had been.

The company had a new president, who was perfect for the job—smart and easy to work with, a great guy. He pleaded with me to stay, but it was time for me to sell the stock and embark on a new venture. I began acquiring land and buildings, and created the Silverman Family Partnerships, developing commercial real estate in the Central Bucks area.

It was a smart move.

CHAPTER 22

Ann and the Life of Our Family

For sixty-five years, from our marriage in 1942 until Ann's death in 2007, Ann was my wife, my helpmeet, my inspiration, my beloved. She was an amazing mother to our four daughters and equally wonderful with our seven grandchildren. Her legacy is her family and also her civic involvements. Ann was someone who always wanted the best for everyone, someone who worked hard to make things better for others. A self-described humanist, she lived her values.

I don't hope to do her justice in this chapter, but I'll try to show something about how central she was to my life and the life of our family. I want to start with the end (which isn't really the end, because her legacy continues), and work backward.

I began grieving for Ann several years before she died. Although we didn't have a diagnosis until a few months before her death, it had been obvious for some time that she was seriously ill. She and I were as much in love as ever, and it was heartbreaking to see her struggle with pain, her active life limited by her illnesses. Our efforts focused on keeping her as free of pain as possible.

For about three years before she died, Ann was in almost constant pain in her back. One of our doctor friends, an anesthesiologist, would come to the house to give her spinal injections, which would help but only for a little while. Several acupuncturists treated her; she thought for a while that the first one had helped. The pain came and went; sometimes she didn't feel pain at all. She did, however, develop other unexplained problems, which were treated symptomatically.

But then Ann got sick, really sick. She wasn't eating. She was retaining water. The hospital admitted her for observation. Her doctor wanted to draw the water out with a needle. Ann resisted until a close friend, the head of the hospital, convinced her it was necessary.

I don't know whether she was more scared of the needle or of what the lab would find.

Some water was removed and sent to the lab. The next morning I had a call from her doctor. The diagnosis was clear: Ann had ovarian cancer. It was shocking news to get over the telephone. I had never suspected that the pain she had been experiencing for more than two years was caused by ovarian cancer, which is hard to detect and which she'd never been tested for. The whole family was shocked, and apparently so were the doctors, but strangely, Ann didn't seem surprised.

We made an appointment with the head cancer specialist at the cancer center at the Doylestown Hospital, which ironically Ann had played an important part in bringing to Doylestown. Our daughter Binny came with us. The doctor looked at the x-rays and lab results, and said there was no point in treatment. He told us to take her home and keep her comfortable. On the way out, Binny took the doctor aside and asked him how long her mother would live. "Three to four months," he said.

During those last months, we watched over her in bed.

Our housekeeper took care of her all day; her daughter, a nurse, came each night to catheterize her, and a great-niece of Ann's helped out as needed. When she was put to bed at nine o'clock, I would get into the bed with her, hug her, and talk to her about how wonderful our life together had been. I would stay with her until she fell asleep.

The hardest moment was when she asked me, in a low voice, "Can you make me well?" I couldn't answer her. It was the first time I couldn't give her whatever she asked for.

I would spend the rest of the night in a chair beside her bed, mostly watching over her, sleeping some, crying and crying. Writing this more than five years later, I'm tearing up.

The idea of being in the house when she died was unbearable. I was overwhelmed with grief. I started to look at apartments and actually put deposits down on two of them and ordered furniture. I canceled the leases and furniture order. I couldn't stand being there when Ann died, but neither could I follow through with a plan to escape.

Three months after her cancer was diagnosed, Ann died. It was two days before Christmas. The whole family was there. We gathered in our bedroom, some of the grandchildren sitting on the floor. Ann seemed barely conscious, if at all, but I think she was aware of all of us being together and being with her. I also think she waited until we'd gone out for dinner before she died. It would have been just like her to want to spare us her last moments.

We rushed home when we got the call. Ann was lying peacefully. Two hours later, after we called the University of Pennsylvania, two people from the funeral home removed her body; consistent with her selflessness and generous spirit, she had donated her remains to the hospital to be used in teaching medical students.

As I said, I started grieving a few years before Ann died, and I still grieve for her despite my happiness in my later marriage to Liz. Ann will always have her place in my heart. I will always miss her.

Let me talk about the legacy she left. First, there's our wonderful family. She raised our daughters to be close to each other. She offered them unconditional approval, encouragement, and support. When they were young, she served as a room mother in their schools. Although she had strong opinions on just about everything, instead of advice she gave them confidence in their choices.

Next was what she did for others. She never saw someone in need whom she didn't try to help. When our daughters were in school, they often brought their friends home, some of them in need of Ann's nurturing and guidance. Ann was generous with her time and advice. As a 4-H club leader, she mentored many young people. Later she organized a Great Books club, providing all the books and offering a place for those who hungered for meaningful discussion to gather.

In Palm Beach one of the security staff in our building confided to Ann that she dreamed of becoming a real estate agent but lacked the money to take the necessary courses and test. Ann subsidized the woman's dream, and the woman passed her courses and test and was able to support her young daughter far better than she could have as a security guard. That is only one example of the many individuals she helped.

Next were her community volunteerism and philanthropy. Ann was active with the Village Improvement Association, the organization that had started and was still running the Doylestown Hospital. There she became aware of unmet health needs of hundreds of the poorer members of our community. She accepted our friend Dr. Dan's challenge to help him start a free clinic at the hospital, staffed by volunteer doctors, nurses, and dentists. She was such a key part of the clinic's success that it was named in her honor: the Ann Silverman Community Health Clinic.

Ann also gave generously of her time and resources to causes including Planned Parenthood, Gilda's Club, the League of Women Voters, the Mercer Museum, the Network of Victim Assistance, the Bucks County Historical Society, and the Bucks County Community College Foundation. In West Palm Beach she helped create a shelter for women and children who needed to escape a violent home situation.

She set an inspiring example of community service few have equaled.

In 2003 the Central Bucks Chamber of Commerce gave Ann a Lifetime Achievement Award as humanitarian.

Ann was Jewish, she was a pacifist, and she was an atheist. Every year we celebrated Passover, and our daughters grew up embracing their Jewish identity, though they had no formal instruction or participation in Judaism. As a humanist Ann was an advocate for peace; she attributed war to the evils of capitalism. She did value money but only insofar as she could give it away to help people for worthy causes. Her beliefs were ethically grounded. She believed human beings are capable of being good without having to rely on a deity or superhuman aid.

While she was known for her kindness and for forbidding any judgmental remarks around her, Ann could be outspoken and sometimes blunt. When our friend Jim Michener defended the legitimacy of censorship, for instance, she harangued him until he changed his mind. She spoke up in meetings when she felt others were pursuing an insignificant topic or approaching a topic in a misguided way. And when she would see someone smoking a cigarette, regardless of whether she knew the person, she would tell him or her to quit.

Of course, many of my best memories are about our children: when they were born, as they grew up, and when they made us grandparents. But some of my best memories are of Ann and me alone. We often traveled alone after the kids grew up, but sometimes we took time just for us while they were still young. When I reminisce about my lifetime of memorable events, one of my favorite memories is of the time we went to Grossinger's Resort in the Catskills without the children for kind of a second honeymoon. We entered a dance contest, and we won!

CHAPTER 23

My Third Miracle

A few days after Ann died, I had heart surgery to replace a valve. I already knew I would need a stent, but I had postponed the surgery because I needed to be available to Ann twenty-four hours a day. Suddenly it became urgent. I was experiencing chest pains—not surprising considering that my heart had just been broken—but the pain was so bad that I woke my daughter Leda and her husband Michael to drive me to the emergency room.

Instead of a stent, I needed a valve replacement. The heart surgeon, knowing I was Jewish, promised me a cow valve. The operation went well, and a few days later I went home. By then the family had dispersed except for my daughter Leda and her husband Michael. With the help of a cousin and the housekeeper, they watched me closely, and a visiting nurse came daily to check my vital signs. All seemed fine until one day the cousin noticed I was slurring my speech and not making any sense.

They called an ambulance and followed it to the hospital, where a CAT scan showed my brain was filling up with blood. The new valve had been pumping hard, and because of the blood thinner, a vein had ruptured in my head. Doylestown Hospital administered a dose of vitamin K and immediately sent me to Abington Hospital, where there were neurologists and neurosurgeons. There I was taken off blood thinners, two holes were drilled through my skull, and I was put into a bed with my feet up and head down so the blood would drain.

I was out of it, but I learned that my daughters took turns visiting me every day and consulted regularly with my doctors, making sure my medical care was the best. It must have been a scary time for them, their mother dying only a few weeks earlier and now expecting to lose their remaining parent—me. There was little hope that I would live, much less recover. In fact, one of the nurses advised my daughters to "make arrangements." The word on the street was that I wasn't going to make it.

Much to everyone's surprise and my family's relief, I didn't die.

Months later I met a doctor from Abington who'd read my scans while I was in the hospital. He said he hadn't expected me to survive. And when I thanked the surgeon for saving my life, telling him my daughters had been scared, he said he too had been scared.

I will always be grateful for my family for the way they kept vigil; for my doctor nephew, who consulted with the head doctor to make some changes in my treatment; and for the brain surgeon.

Whenever I hear people bad-mouthing immigrants, I tell them about my surgeon and about how lucky I am that he came to America from the Philippines and saved my life.

I'm beginning to believe that my luck will hold. Surviving my birth was the first miracle, and being saved when I was choking on the peach pit was the second. Surviving and recovering from the brain bleed was the third, and there may be more miracles ahead.

CHAPTER 24

....

Liz

While I was still recovering from the brain hemorrhage, I decided to start dating. I went out with several women acquaintances and soon realized what I wanted was a serious, committed relationship. I'd been happily married to Ann for more than six decades, and I liked being married. Most men my age would be looking for companionship. This eighty-eight-year-old man knew he wanted to be married, passionately and happily, to an extraordinary woman.

Shortly after my discharge from the hospital, I saw Liz in a restaurant, and I remembered that when we had both been on the Bucks County arts council, she had been the liveliest member. I invited her to lunch in a small restaurant near her office.

As soon as we were seated, I informed her in a loud voice that I intended to see more of her, because she had "nice tits," had "a nice ass" and shared my mother's name. I told her, still in a loud voice, that I hadn't had sex in a long time but that she would find I had all the inclinations and abilities of a young man. "I know how to make a woman love me," I said.

The restaurant was packed, mostly with people who knew both Liz and me. As I spoke the restaurant went completely quiet. Several people came over to our table to say hello. They obviously were amused. Liz wasn't.

During the lunch I asked Liz about her plans for the evening. She said she was going to the opening of a Quaker art show. I had no special interest in Quaker art, but I surprised her there, and after a few minutes of looking around, I offered to buy her any piece of art she liked. She declined. I then invited her to dinner, promising her the best dinner she'd ever eaten. She declined. I took her gently by the wrist and led her out to my car, illegally parked behind the building, and drove her to a small café in Stockton, New Jersey.

Now, this café is the kind of place that still serves baked beans with ham hocks. I had come to like their soup and side dishes. I informed Liz that Ann and I had often eaten here and that we'd always shared our dinners. Then I ordered a cup—not a bowl—of cabbage soup and two potato-onion pancakes, which I drenched in imitation maple syrup. Liz chose not to accept my offer to share the meal, so I ate it all myself.

On the way back to Doylestown, Liz asked me whether my car had turn signals and whether it stopped for stop signs. I think she was trying to tell me she didn't like my driving, but she was nice about it, as she had been about dinner. She was so nice that I asked her to go out with me again the next night. I was hoping for a second chance.

She made it clear that she had no interest in a romantic relationship with me or with anyone else but that she would be happy to be my friend, perhaps the best friend I had ever had. I told her that if it was a friend I was looking for, I would get a dog.

Lucky for me, Liz did agree to go on a second date. This time I took her to one of the finest restaurants in the area. What I didn't know until much later was that when I excused myself to go to the bathroom, the maître d' went over to the table, leaned down toward her face, glared at her, and hissed, "I loved Ann, you know."

For our third date, Liz invited me to "Liz's Diner," a weekly event in her condo, in which she cooked dinner for some special friends. By then I'd made up my mind that I would marry her, not something I said out loud, but I did announce to her friends that they would be seeing less of her, as I intended to monopolize her time and that I had a plan to "put her in a palace." Two of her friends were charmed. They noted that I was obviously "smitten." A third friend was upset because he thought I would try to dominate and control Liz. Fat chance of that!

Soon after our first weeks of seeing each other, Liz went on a cruise to Alaska with her sister and six friends, a trip she had booked months before. During the eight days when she was away, I missed her terribly. I would call her cell phone or have her paged shore to ship. When she returned, I informed her that we were going to get married. "Get used to it, kid, because it is going to happen."

Liz asked me to wait until a year had passed since Ann's death before suggesting marriage. But I'm not a patient man, and I had a plan.

I bought a large condo in the complex where Liz lived, and I presented her with a choice: she could move in with me, or she could come home from work to find her condo empty, with a note telling her all her possessions were now in my new home. Either way, I intended to buy her condo and sell it right away so she would have to live with me. And because I'm a traditional man, if we were going to live together, we would have to get married.

"Ask me on your birthday in January," she said. "I'll be willing to talk to you about it then."

"What will your answer be?"

"Probably yes. You know I really do adore you."

"OK, good enough, but if we are going to get engaged in January, let's look at rings now so we can find what we want. I have a jeweler friend who has nice diamonds."

Liz said she didn't want a diamond for environmental, political, and social reasons. She said she would prefer a sapphire.

Jewish husbands give their fiancées diamonds, not sapphires.

I arranged with my friend Eddie, the jeweler, to meet us at his shop, and I coached him on what he was to do and say. When Liz asked to see his sapphires, he shook his head sorrowfully and told her it was almost impossible to find nice sapphires anymore. He pulled out a tray with four or five very sorry-looking stones. Then he said he understood Liz's reservations about diamonds but mentioned casually that he had some that were certified as responsibly mined. Liz agreed that one of the ones he showed her was lovely, but she insisted that she didn't want a diamond, and since January was still six months away, surely he could find an acceptable sapphire by then. Eddie said he would start looking and suggested he measure her finger so when he found a good sapphire, he could have it mounted so she could see how it looked on her hand.

Two days later I picked up the diamond ring Eddie had prepared and presented it to Liz. She was surprised but already starting to get used to the idea that when I have a plan, I make it happen. (And I did design and have made for her a sapphire ring, which I gave her on our second wedding anniversary.)

The next step of my plan was to convince her to marry me right after Christmas.

Liz had insisted that we not get engaged until the Yahrzeit of Ann's death, but now that I had tricked her into accepting an engagement ring and since I had manipulated her into moving in with me, she realized that sooner or later I got what I wanted, so she had just as well go along with my plan.

Liz was concerned about how my family would feel about us having a wedding barely a year after losing their mother. To show respect she decided to keep her own name. "There was a Mrs. Silverman, and let's retire that name with her." She also insisted that our wedding would be idiosyncratic, serious, and lighthearted—classical music and a Quaker bluegrass band, a casual midday event rather than a formal evening affair.

The guest list was huge because my family is huge, and there were lots of her family who would want to be there, plus each of us had some close friends. We booked the Doylestown Country Club, planned a menu that considered gluten and dairy sensitivities in my family and vegetarian and vegan regimens in both families, and invited 140 people.

One of my sons-in-law gifted us with a paint-by-number piece of artwork; he had developed a system for parties and special occasions in which attenders at events colored in lines he put on canvas. A friend of Liz's came up from Washington, DC, to play Bach before the ceremony. The Quaker bluegrass band, most of whom were Liz's friends, provided the rest of the music, including what we had chosen as "our" song, "I Can See Clearly Now." We brought in a square dance caller. A Wiccan friend would lead a Starhawk spiral dance.

The minister, a close friend who'd led interfaith congregations after leaving his Methodist ministry, performed the ceremony. He incorporated Jewish references into his welcoming remarks. Liz cried when we said our vows and exchanged rings. I gave her my handkerchief. One of my granddaughters brought forward a glass wrapped in a napkin. I broke the glass, and we were married.

We came home from the wedding to get ready to leave the next morning for a honeymoon cruise. I was carrying in the remains of the wedding cake, although Liz had told me she would do it. I snapped at her—the first time ever— and tripped coming in from the garage.

I snapped at her again when she insisted I should go to the emergency room. Not an auspicious beginning of what would be a wonderful marriage.

A nephew and his wife had missed the wedding because they'd thought it was in the evening, so they had just arrived in the vicinity when they called us. The nephew is a doctor. Liz asked him to come over right away. He persuaded me to get an x-ray. I had broken a bone in my rear end and was admitted. We spent our wedding night apart. Liz canceled our honeymoon plans. She was nice about it, although for a while she stayed upset at the way I had yelled at her.

In the weeks following the wedding, after four or five days in the hospital, I was confined to a bed in the downstairs den. On my birthday I was able to come to the table in a wheelchair to have lunch with a few friends, who had been told to bring Jewish jokes instead of gifts. Our moods improved.

Eventually, we would take the honeymoon cruise, which would be the last significant travel we would do.

Engraved in our wedding bands were the words "Isn't it great?"

CHAPTER 25

Living at Pennswood Village

My intention had been to spend the rest of my life getting old in a house in Doylestown with hired caregivers, as needed. Liz didn't like that idea. She wanted us to live in a community where health care was always available and where we would spend time every day with congenial people. She suggested we apply to Pennswood Village, a "continuing care" facility about half an hour from Doylestown. She had put herself on the waiting list many years earlier. Her sister already lived there, and she already knew quite a few of the residents. I hated the prospect of living in an apartment instead of a house, of being half an hour from my hometown, and of losing privacy.

But after meeting several Pennswood residents and attending Liz's sister's birthday party there, I agreed at least to take "the tour." It really wasn't as bad as I had expected. I told Liz I could imagine moving there when I was "old," and I agreed to add my name to hers on the official waiting list. Maybe in two years I would be ready.

Liz had been on the waiting list for such a long time that it was only a few months later that we got a call telling us several apartments were available. Personally, I thought it was premature to look at them, but Liz insisted, so we went, and we looked at five or six apartments. One was too small, and several were too far from the main building, but one would be adequate, I decided, if we removed a wall to make it feel less cramped.

Some people think I'm impetuous. "We'll take it," I said, and we got a move-in date for three months later.

The three months went by. We had reserved a moving van and put the condo on the market; someone had already signed an agreement to buy it. It was three days before moving day. I changed my mind about going to Pennswood. I told Liz that I would reconsider it in two or three years, that at eighty-nine I wasn't ready to live with old people.

Liz calmly informed me that she was going, with or without me.

"Are you taking the dog?" I had come to love Liz's dog, and he loved me.

"Yes," she said.

"OK, I give in." And so we moved, and by the second day, I was happy that we were living at Pennswood. I got to know the people Liz already knew and met a lot of other people with whom we shared dinners and activities. Mostly I appreciated the fitness facilities and the health care. And when a larger apartment became available, we moved into it, and I was even happier.

I continue to go to my office and my gallery (once that was set up). When I stopped driving at ninety-three, I was able to get to Doylestown by Bucks County Transport, and I found drivers to take me on day-trips on weekends. We also have our second home as a place for me to get away from the old people we live with. My life is different but not confining.

Liz is busy here with committees and special projects. She is appreciative of how administration and staff collaborate with residents' ideas. My participation is mostly socializing in the fitness center and over dinners, and going to the movies, concerts, and presentations offered several times a week.

Our kids are happy that we are taken care of. Both of us have needed to go to the hospital from here. One time after midnight, from the time we called "resident health" until I arrived by ambulance at the nearby hospital, no more than ten or fifteen minutes had gone by. We also appreciate the nonemergency health services, with regular appointments with the doctors and nurse practitioners, checkups, blood work, and coordination of care with our outside specialists. For the health services alone, it was a good move.

I have a good time at dinner with friends. Sometimes I bring up a topic from the news, mostly relating to economic injustice. Sometimes I tell my jokes, even when Liz reminds me that I've already told a particular joke to these people or that this particular joke is inappropriate or not funny. That doesn't stop me, and even when I mess up the punch line, people are kind enough to laugh. Sometimes someone says something that reminds me of a show tune. Then I start singing, and most of the time someone else at our table or nearby will sing with me. Lots of us at Pennswood know the same music.

What surprises me most is that life is easier, more comfortable, and as full or fuller than ever. When a light bulb burns out or something needs fixing, I make a call or Liz fills out a form, and Maintenance takes care of it. Pennswood drivers take us to our off-site medical appointments and bring us back. Our apartment is warm in the winter and cool in the summer. I exercise three times a week in our wonderful fitness center without having to leave the premises. Our kids and grandkids visit. The dog thrives with all the attention he gets. We have a social life here, and we still go out with friends from the "outside."

Isn't it great?

CHAPTER 26

Second Homes

For many years Ann and I spent the winter months in Palm Beach, Florida. Now I was living full-time in a retirement community, and I was restless—restless and wanting to be around people of different ages. It was time to get a second home.

At first I imagined buying a property in Ashville after reading a magazine article about how nice it was there, but traveling had become difficult, if not impossible. I realized I needed to find a place closer to home, one that didn't require air travel.

On our first anniversary, being the good husband that I am, I asked Liz whether she was happy. "Yes," she said.

"Really happy?"

"Yes, really happy."

"Really, really happy?"

"Yes, really, really happy."

"Is there anything you can think of that you want? Anything that might make you even happier?"

"Well, I do get homesick for Greenport."

Liz had spent eleven years in Greenport before returning to Bucks County. Greenport is a small fishing village on the North Fork of Long Island. Liz had worked there in the drug and alcohol field, as a counselor, as a community organizer and project director, and as chair of the zoning board. She had many close friends there, five of whom had come to our wedding.

I really am a good husband. I didn't hesitate. "Let's get a second home there." I meant it. I knew Greenport from visiting there with my family and from accompanying Liz to a memorial service there. And if it would add to Liz's happiness, I would buy her a house in Greenport.

Liz immediately started checking listings online on a realtor friend's website. A cottage caught her attention. It was a Sears kit house—very small but charming and the right price. I called the realtor to set up a meeting and see the house two weeks later. Two weeks and four hours later, we had an agreement of sale.

It had one bathroom, one small bedroom, one closet-sized bedroom, and a small living/dining space—and almost immediately I became claustrophobic. We hired a contractor to turn the tiny bedroom into a bathroom and build an addition with a large bedroom and bath.

We settled in, and I mostly liked being there, but a year or so later I realized I didn't like it enough to spend a lot of time there. We listed the house, and it sold quickly.

Meanwhile, I still felt that I needed a second home. Liz reminded me that I'd often spoken about my childhood fantasy of having a place on Rittenhouse Square. She said that I had "done" Greenport for her, and now it was my turn. We found a one-bedroom apartment with partial views of Rittenhouse Square and fixed it up a bit. Once in a while we would go into Philadelphia for a day or two, sometimes three, but only occasionally, and all our sojourns there required us to kennel the dog.

I decided after a year to sell the apartment and buy a beach house at the Jersey Shore. I liked what I had heard about Avalon By the Sea. Liz didn't share my enthusiasm for a beach house, reminding me that neither of us can sit in the sun and that we wouldn't find friends or a sense of community there. But if I went down to check it out and saw something I really liked, she would at least look at it. So I went down with a friend, looked around, and gradually realized that, while a beach house in Avalon By the Sea didn't offer what we were looking for, Greenport did.

As soon as I walked into the apartment from the scouting expedition, without even saying hello to Liz, I went to the phone and called our realtor friend in Greenport. "Dave? We made a mistake. We never should have left Greenport. Do you have a house for us?"

Three days later we looked at five listings and made an offer on the house I thought was perfect (it had a fenced yard for our dog, Sammy, and a sunroom for me). Our offer was accepted within hours, and we had a second home again.

Unfortunately, the house was in terrible condition. I didn't mind the house as it was, but Liz insisted on making it habitable and beautiful. We still had furniture from the bungalow and the apartment. Our contractor friend and our housepainter friend, who had worked on our bungalow, got to work with electricians, plumbers, landscapers, and others.

By the way, I've always warned people about doing business with friends. I take it back. When you're part of a community and have friends who are excellent at what they do, you should always do business with them when you can.

I like it so much in Greenport in this house, and Liz is so happy here that we spend three weeks out of every three months here year-round. We even got to experience Hurricane Sandy here—snug and warm and safe in our little house, never losing power and never experiencing damage to the house. And when it snows, our contractor friend sends his crew to dig us out.

Life is good.

CHAPTER 27

My Love Affair with Art

When I was twelve years old, we lived only a mile from the Philadelphia Art Museum, not much farther from the Rodin Museum.

Admission was free. I would go with friends on weekends, where we would spend many hours fascinated by the art. I was most intrigued by the size of some of the paintings, by the portraits of European royalty, by the many battle scenes, and by the landscapes. I was also fascinated with the life-size statue of a horse with a rider dressed in full armor, the first thing I would see when coming into the museum.

Art made me aware that there was a world beyond Strawberry Mansion, beyond the world I'd been born into. And already being committed to being wealthy myself someday, I got a feel for rich people donating art for the public to appreciate.

Early in our marriage, Ann and I began to collect paintings, mostly Bucks County Impressionist art from what was known as the New Hope School. Art was affordable in those days, with many recognized and lesser-known artists painting all along the Delaware River. It didn't take long for us to fill every room of our house with paintings.

Bucks County was well known for its art, yet there was no place to see it and no effort on the part of county officials to promote it. But then we elected an artist as a county commissioner, a remarkable man named Denver Lindley. Denver persuaded the commissioners to set up an arts council to promote the arts of Bucks County. It would be an official member of county government. The commissioners appointed me chairman. For several years we held meetings in the office of one of the commissioners.

Our original charge from the commissioners was to manage government-funded artwork to be installed in county government buildings.

The arts council had about ten individuals on it, all of them interesting, accomplished people, several of them artists. Meetings were lively. Creative ideas flew around the room. It was also the setting in which I got to know Liz better; I thought she was the liveliest member of our group.

One of the early projects of the council was to set up an art mobile. We might not yet have a place for people to come see prominent Bucks County art, but we could bring art to the people. We persuaded the Strick Trailer Company to donate a trailer, the owner of the local daily paper to outfit it, and a local bank to fund a curator for five years. We had acquired some great art by that time, art that had been sitting in a closet in one of the public schools in the county.

The art mobile would go from school to school, spending one month at each school and bringing art education to the children. During the summer the art mobile would be open to the public in parking lots around the county. It now belongs to the Bucks County Community College, and it continues to bring art and art education to the schools.

We still needed a permanent place to show and expand our collection of Bucks County art. When the Bucks County Prison moved to a new facility, I told the county commissioners I wanted the old building; what's more, I wanted them to give us $1 million to build our museum there. They agreed. The arts council decided to give the museum a recognizable name; we named it after my good friend James Michener. The arts council morphed into the board of directors for the Michener Museum, with me as chair.

My friend Jim Michener had predicted the project would fail. He was mistaken. The museum, much expanded, has more than one hundred thirty-five thousand visitors a year. It owns an impressive collection of Bucks County art and hosts about fifteen special exhibitions each year. I remain chairman emeritus for life.

For a long time I'd been interested in promoting local living artists who continued to work in the New Hope tradition. I spent a year visiting galleries on both sides of the Delaware River and talking with artists about their needs and wants. "Wall space," they all told me, a place to hang their art for longer than they could in typical gallery shows. And publicity, they said, and enough money to make a living.

So that was the challenge: could I establish a gallery, support local artists, and at least break even? We started with four artists, now seven, all exhibiting their work year-round, and we're featuring the individual artists each year with special openings. With permanent wall space and publicity, all the artists are doing well, and many people see and buy their work, enriching their homes and offices with Bucks County art. I feel privileged to accomplish this, even if the gallery isn't breaking even.

Years ago I took a one-day course in sculpture, and I made a piece that, in my opinion, is perfect. Now I'm trying my hand at art once more. I'm experimenting with drawing, mastering perspective and free form. I'm having fun seeing that I can still learn new techniques.

Watch for a show of my drawings in about ten years from now!

CHAPTER 28

Retrospection: No Regrets, No Shame, and No Resentments

What a funny life I've lived. It sounds strange to be almost ninety-five and have no regrets. I grew up as a socialist, a socialist who felt a commitment to doing the right thing, one who was aware from childhood of injustice and inequality. That hasn't changed.

In all my personal relationships and in business, I've treated people with respect, consideration, and caring.

When I was a little boy, my mother told me to put a penny into a collection cup for orphans in Africa. I asked her whether there really were children poorer than we were. "Yes," she said. It was a lesson I remembered all my life.

The other message she instilled in me was never to shame her in front of the neighbors. "Whatever you do," she would tell me, "do not bring a *shonda* to me."

My sense of what is shameful has evolved over time, so now I think in terms of myself, not of my mother or the neighbors; and I can't think of anything I need to make amends for.

What's more, I don't waste energy judging others or holding grudges.

Yes, I feel outrage: I wonder whether the super-wealthy, with their displays of conspicuous consumption, their self-indulgence and their sense of entitlement, feel ashamed when they think of people who have so much less than they do, the millions of people who cannot even meet their basic needs. What is worse, they seem to resist anything that would mean sharing their wealth, that would help those who have less than they do. Personally, I think they should feel deep shame.

What about me? you ask. What about my having so much wealth when so many people have so little? I don't need to feel any shame around my wealth, because I used so much of it to do good in the community and beyond. As a Jewish husband and father, the financial security of my family was a priority. So was contributing money and time to causes and organizations that improved people's lives, especially those offering health, housing, and poverty relief as well as cultural and educational programs.

As my wife, Ann, once said, "There is only one good thing about working hard and making money, and that is being able to give it away. Otherwise, it has no value."

CHAPTER 29

Never Better

When I was a young man, I made plans, lots of plans, and believe it or not, I actually have accomplished everything I set out to do. My life is different now: since I'm almost ninety-five years old, it is less focused on accomplishments. Yes, I miss travel, driving, my independence. I wish I still had my excellent memory, my ability to think straight, my agile mind. But I'm still the optimist I've always been, and I can find delight in the people around me, in the activities of a typical day, and in the workings of my imagination.

Yet to be as healthy, active, and happy as I am is truly wonderful. Of course, it would be nice to have another four or five years of the kind of life I have now; it would be a miracle, a welcome one. But my focus now is on the present: enjoying each day; loving my children, grandchildren, and great-grandchildren; learning new things; keeping up with the news; still promoting the arts; and supporting efforts to make things better for other people. Life with

Liz is wonderful, and I love her family. Life at Pennswood Village and in our second home is wonderful. I'm a happy man.

Ask me how I am. I will answer, "Never better."

About the Author

Herman Silverman is an icon, whose life stories and contributions to the common good continue to inspire all who know him. A natural raconteur, Herman has compiled a collection of vignettes spanning the ninety-five years of his life. Founder and long-time president of the nationally known company Sylvan Pools, he was later a managing partner of Silverman Family Partnerships, a commercial real estate management and development company; in 2010 he opened an eponymous art gallery. He helped found the James A. Michener Art Museum, where he holds the title of "chairman for life." For twenty-two years he served on the Pennsylvania Housing Finance Agency, and he has been a significant source of support for numerous human services and arts organizations in Bucks County, Pennsylvania.

He lives with his wife, Elizabeth Serkin, and their dog, named Sammy in honor of his father in Pennswood Village, a continuing-care retirement community in Newtown, Pennsylvania.